Print & Pattern 2
Bowie Style

LAURENCE KING

Published in 2011 by

Laurence King Publishing Ltd
361–373 City Road
London EC1V 1LR
United Kingdom
Tel: +44 20 7841 6900
Fax: +44 20 7841 6910
email: enquiries@laurenceking.com
www.laurenceking.com

A catalogue record for this book is
available from the British Library.

ISBN 978-1-85669-792-7

Book and cover design: & SMITH
www.andsmithdesign.com

Printed in China.

Inside cover:
Pop Floral by Rachel Cave

Contents

Above /
A selection of greeting
cards by Marie Perkins.

Introduction
Marie Perkins

a.k.a. Bowie Style
www.printpattern.blogspot.com

The world is full of patterns – on curtains, wallpaper, greeting cards, stationery and tableware – but only rarely are you able to find out who designed them. The website Print & Pattern loves to shine a light on the designers behind the patterns, so I was delighted when Laurence King Publishing approached me to curate a new book and showcase a fresh selection of fantastic designers. In this volume I believe I have brought together some of the most talented freelance surface designers working today.

Pattern is a powerful tool that can transform a mundane product into a statement of taste and style. It can build brands through memorable motifs and signature prints. Also, choosing a pattern that reflects their own personality is a means of individual expression for consumers.

Most of the designers in this book are available for commissions. So, if you like their work, drop them a line – I am sure they would be delighted to hear from you!

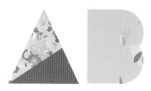

Abigail Brown

www.abigail-brown.co.uk
www.mysugarcube.com
abigailbrown81@hotmail.co.uk

01 // Abigail Brown has a degree in Surface Decoration and Printed Textiles and is currently based in London. Her work is inspired by children's books and toys, vintage design and illustration, Japanese character design, and nature. Abigail's past clients have included Marks & Spencer, Mamas & Papas, Sainsbury's Tu range and John Lewis.

Design Heroes:
Donna Wilson, Nathalie Lete, Marc Boutavant.

Above / Summer
Created for the design studio My Sugar Cube this confetti-like design of leaves has tremendous detail in each motif.

Opposite / Bloom
Created in Adobe Illustrator with layers of built-up texture, this pattern uses a sophisticated but fresh colour palette.

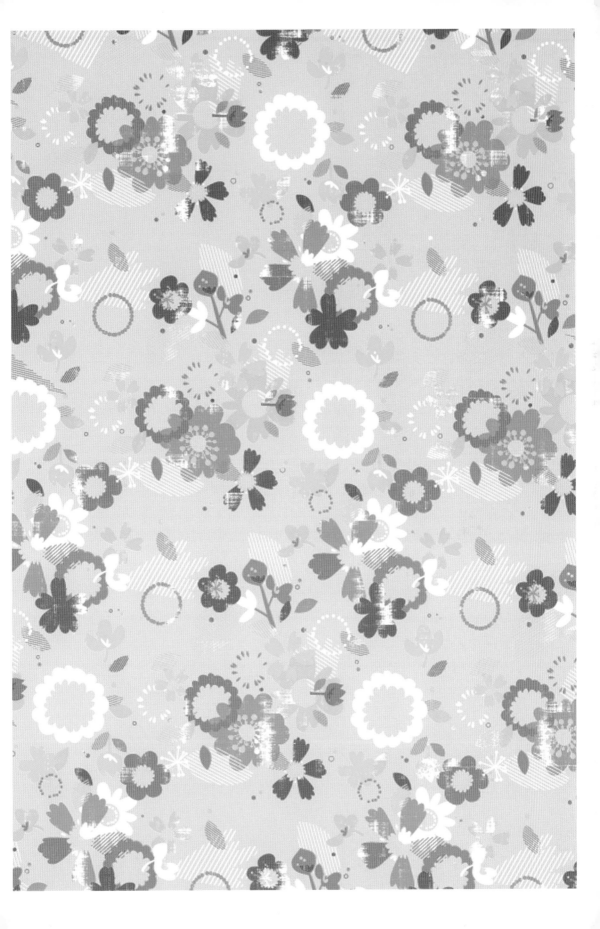

Aimee Wilder

www.aimeewilder.com
www.aimeewilder.bigcartel.com
info@aimeewilder.com

02 // Aimee Wilder grew up in New York City, in both the Bronx and Midtown Manhattan, but is now based in Williamsburg, Brooklyn. She studied Art and Technology at The Art Institute of Chicago, and prior to that Fine Art and Architecture at Hobart and William Smith Colleges in Geneva (NY). Before launching her own branded label Aimee worked as an in-house designer for Dwell Studio and Martha Stewart Living. She has also designed for Vans, Urban Outfitters, Crate & Barrel and Gap Kids. Aimee's influences include graffiti art, urban toy design, Swiss graphic design and Japanese art and culture. Now creating her own wallpapers and pillows Aimee says her break into home decor was with Christiane Lemieux and Jenna Chused at Dwell Studio, and she has always wanted to thank them. She is now keen to work on large scale conceptual art installations.

Design Heroes:
David Hicks, Klaus Oldenberg, Verner Panton and Eero Aarnio.

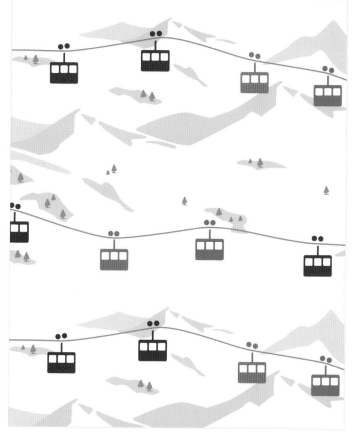

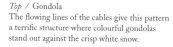

Top / Gondola
The flowing lines of the cables give this pattern a terrific structure where colourful gondolas stand out against the crisp white snow.

Bottom left / Sugar Cookie
Geometrics meet florals in this 'one design does all' pattern.

Bottom right / Tulip Stripe
Inspired by retro pattern design of the 1960s this striped layout benefits from a striking colour palette.

Opposite / Analog Nights
Aimee collected images of analog music equipment and created this design using Adobe Illustrator and scanned photographs. It has proved very popular as wallpaper.

Opposite / Splash
These triangles and angular lines, softened by dots, were inspired by 1980s graphics and patterns.

Above / Dino Repeat
Created for children's bedding, this classic boys' design was inspired by vintage dinosaur colouring books.

Allihopa

www.allihopa.co.uk
www.allihopalovesyou.blogspot.com
post@allihopa.co.uk

03 // Allihopa is formed of Mrs Richardson (aka Lucy), and Mrs Flynn (aka Malin) and together they create greeting cards, gift wrap and other paper goods, which they claim mix both of their creative roots: 'British eccentricity with Scandinavian cool'. Malin is originally from Lund in Sweden and studied graphic design in Los Angeles. Lucy is from Wales and following studies in Contour Fashion Design at De Montfort University worked in the fashion industry. The duo met when they worked as design advisors to the Welsh fashion industry and decided to set up Allihopa (Swedish for 'everybody') and jump out of the corporate box. They now hope to expand Allihopa into home and fashion accessories as well as continuing the social stationery they love.

Design Heroes:
Paul Smith, Kate Spade.

Top / Birgit
A design created for a greeting card collection called Maj-Mai – after the Swedish and Welsh words for the month of May – that was launched in July 2010. This design is a kaleidoscopic story of a midnight orchard garden featuring quirky characters and eye-catching stripes.

Bottom / Blodwyn
In this Maj-Mai design Allihopa tried to create something a bit less cute than their previous designs and play around with overlays to create a kaleidoscopic effect.

Top / Tweetprint
Created especially to be a cute and colourful art print suitable for a child's bedroom or the kidult market, this design features characters from all of Allihopa's different collections.

Middle left / Greta
Also in the Maj-Mai series, this design, like all the others in the series, sports a person's first name.

Middle right / Iolo
Bold shapes and adventurous brights are set against a dramatic dark background.

Bottom / Eskil
Allihopa have also turned Eskil into an art print in which the Eskil character features with his girlfriend, Gwendolen. All the designs start out as simple hand-sketches that are finished in Illustrator.

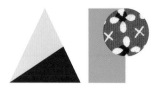

Alys Paterson

www.alyspaterson.com
alyspaterson.blogspot.com
alys@alyspaterson.com

04 // Alys Paterson is based
in the creative hub that is Bristol,
having moved there after
graduating with a degree in
Illustration from University
College Falmouth. Her work is a
beautiful combination of hand-
painting, collage and computer
design, and she draws inspiration
from a love of Scandinavian design,
illustrators from the 1950s and '60s,
and the books she had when she
was a child. Clients have included
Habitat, John Lewis, Waterstone's
and Anorak. All the designs
featured here were licensed for
greeting cards by The Art Group.
In the future, she would love to
illustrate picture books of her own.

Design Heroes:
Alexander Girard, Stig Lindberg,
Tove Jansson, Miroslav Sasek, Rob
Ryan, Mary Blair.

Top / Little Leaves
This design suggests the
beginning of autumn when
the leaves are just beginning
to change.

Bottom / Heartsong
Based on a concept of birds
singing love songs to each
other, the heart motif provides
the perfect frame for a burst
of illustration.

Top / My Love Grows
Alys captures the spirit of love blossoming and growing in front of your eyes by turning the heart motif into an organic plant-like design.

Bottom left / Paris Park
In Alys's mind Parisian parks are full of balloon sellers and carousels. The opacity of the balloons adds real depth to the image.

Bottom right /
Esther's Big Day
Inspired by the numerous weddings Alys has attended, the cheerful bunting provides a great opportunity for using colour and pattern.

Amy Blay

www.amyblay.com
www.lillarogers.com
amyblay@blueyonder.co.uk

05 // Born in Montreal, Amy studied for an Illustration degree at London's University of Westminster and a master's degree in Communication Design at Central Saint Martins. Now based in Cheltenham, Amy works on all kinds of freelance design and illustration projects and is represented by Lilla Rogers. Clients have included The Art Group, Card Mix, Galison/ Mudpuppy, Graham & Brown, Hallmark UK, Nouvelles Images, Papyrus, Penguin, Publications International, UK Greetings, and Woodmansterne. Amy is inspired by vintage posters, toys, album covers, maps, packaging, fabric, children's books, the Golden Books series, Japanese *zakka*, Scandinavian design, car boot finds, and children's animation. Her dream commission would be to write and illustrate her own children's books.

Design Heroes:
Jim Flora, Mary Blair, J. Otto Seibold, Miroslav Sasek, Alice & Martin Provensen, Dick Bruna, Tove Jansson.

Above / Nursery Walk
Like all of Amy's designs, this delightful print was created in Adobe Illustrator. It features a myriad of cute characters woven together by the device of a winding white road. Originally designed for a personal fabric project, this has since been used as a greeting card by Cafe Press.

Top / Rainbow Zoo
– Birthday Bear
A speculative card design that was retro-inspired and incorporates an ageing effect to make the image look worn. The balance is perfect between the bear, geometric balloons and interesting fonts.

Middle / Rainbow Zoo
– Elephant
A vintage style greeting card design published by Card Mix. Added interest and depth comes from the elephant's patterned ear, while the mouse gives the image a fun dynamic.

Bottom / Rainbow Zoo
– Wrap
The zoo is a perennial favourite in children's design but Amy's style and riot of colours gives it a modern update. This design is used on stationery and fabric by Otto Trading/Red Rooster Fabrics.

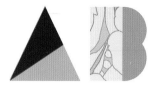

Amy Butler

www.amybutlerdesign.com

06 // Amy Butler is a creative designer known for her sophisticated yet relaxed modern approach to printed fabrics and products for home, fashion and craft. As a sewing pattern designer, she has brought modern styling to the sewing arts and inspired a new generation of young women to 'find their own style'. With millions of hits a month on her website and numerous editorial appearances, Amy's growing brand has become synonymous with creativity, sustainability, quality and great style. Amy works from her studio in Central Ohio with her husband, cats and a small staff of amazing friends. Her fabrics, patterns, handbags, home decor products and project books are sold worldwide.

Opposite top /
Water Garden Forest
A licensed design for
Rowan fabric from the
Daisy Chain Collection.
Japanese style blossoms
and chrysanthemums are
illustrated in a calming
minty green palette.

Opposite bottom /
Wallflower Sky
A licensed design for
Rowan fabric from the Lotus
Collection, it features a
mandala in a bold repeat.

Above /
Dream Poppies (Seafoam)
A licensed design for Rowan
fabric from the August
Fields Collection featuring
yellow flowers outlined for
extra definition and superb
detailing.

Overleaf /
Imperial Fans (River)
A licensed design for Rowan
fabric from the Nigella
Collection which cleverly
manages to look both classical
and contemporary.

Page 24 /
Lacework Midnight
Created by Amy Butler
and licensed as wallpaper
for Graham & Brown,
this delicate lace looks
stunning against the dark
blue background.

Page 25 /
Memento Midnight
This folk floral style
design was also created
by Amy Butler and
licensed as wallpaper
for Graham & Brown.

Opposite / Lacework (Midnight)
Created by Amy Butler and licensed as wallpaper for Graham
& Brown, this delicate lace looks stunning against the dark
blue background.

Above / Memento (Midnight)
This folk floral style design was created by Amy Butler
and licensed as wallpaper for Graham & Brown.

Amy King

www.shinyorangedreams.blogspot.com
www.spoonflower.com/profiles/amel24
amel97@earthlink.net

07 //   Amy King grew up in London but has been living in New York for many years. She studied Textile Design at the Fashion Institute of Technology in New York and has worked as a fabric designer for BabyGap and Martha Stewart Living amongst others. Amy's designs have also been purchased by an array of companies including Target and Paperchase and she is always interested in new design commissions, especially in the greeting card and gift wrap markets.

Design Heroes:
Lotta Jansdotter, Marimekko, Jonathan Adler, Lucienne Day.

Top /
Blue and Cream Circles
This design started life as a doodle during a phone call, but then Amy worked it up fully into a stylish monochromatic pattern.

Bottom / Aqua/Lime Floral
A stylized floral which displays influences from 1950s design.

Opposite top /
Happy Smiley Apples
Influenced by the simplicity of Scandinavian design with the addition of a mix of textures and a *kawaii* smile.

Above / Woodland Friends
A whimsical print of little animals meeting in the woods showcases Amy's expertise in children's design.

Above / Sweet Birdhouse
Amy was inspired to create this design for a Spoonflower fabric competition. It has a retro influence but with a playful, modern twist.

Angela Adams

www.angelaadams.com
customerservice@angelaadams.com

o8 // Angela Adams grew up on North Haven, an island 19km (12 miles) off the coast of Maine and is now based in Portland. Angela and her husband, furniture designer Sherwood Hamill, started their modern luxury design company in 1998. Their product range includes rugs, upholstered furniture, fabrics, wallcoverings, carpet, tiles, bedding and bath products, handbags and much more. Angela is inspired by nature, her family, and the dramatic beauty of Maine which resonates throughout all of her work. A combination of nostalgia and modernity have led her to create timeless designs that will blend with all styles of home.

Top / Lulu
Angela is best known for her organic geometric designs that are often inspired by nature. Lulu has a soft soothing aesthetic with no sharp angles.

Bottom /
Correspondence Cards
Organic shapes, bold colours and retro appeal make up this fabulous set of correspondence cards created using some of Angela's best known patterns and published by Chronicle Books.

Opposite /
Manfred Butler Tray
The rounded rectangles were inspired by vintage radios and television sets and the connecting lines represent their antennas.

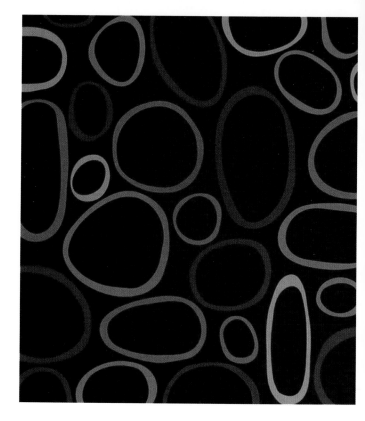

08 / Angela Adams

Opposite / Islands
This pattern was inspired by Maine Islands life. Coastal
style and the landscape have always had a large influence on
Angela's designs.

Above / Birdseed
Inspired by coastal colours, this tea towel represents the
sand and the sea and the songbirds of Maine, in a sunny
illustrative design.

Angie Lewin

www.angielewin.co.uk
www.stjudes.co.uk
info@stjudes.co.uk

09 // Angie Lewin is originally from Cheshire but is now based in Norfolk and the Scottish Highlands. Angie completed a degree in Fine Art Printmaking at the Central School of Art and Design followed by Postgraduate Printmaking at the Camberwell School of Arts and Crafts. Angie's work is inspired by her sketches and photographs of plant forms, a love for the Festival of Britain, and by garden writers Beth Chatto and Christopher Lloyd. She has designed a fabric collection for Liberty, and other clients include the Victoria and Albert Museum, Conran Octopus, Sainsbury's, BBC Publications, Penguin, Dorling Kindersley, Waitrose and, importantly, St. Jude's. In 2010 she released a book of works *Plants & Places* published by Merrell. Accolades include being elected to The Royal Society of Painter Printmakers in 2006, The Society of Wood Engravers in 2008, and The Art Workers Guild in 2010.

Design Heroes:
Eric Ravilious, Lucienne Day, Robert Stewart, Piet Oudolf.

Above / Clifftop Weybourne
A limited edition print from a linocut. Angie is very interested in the structure of plants, particularly seed heads, as this piece shows.

Bottom left / Dandelions 1
Wood engraving and linocut. The seed head of this dandelion takes on a skeletal form for a striking graphic look.

Bottom right / Alliums
A limited edition print from a linocut featuring graphic plant forms in a stylized colour palette.

09 / Angie Lewin

Opposite / Dandelion One (Sage Yellow)
A screen-printed fabric designed for St. Jude's. The curving
flowers look graceful and the textured ground adds depth
and richness.

Above / Hedgerow (Grey/Green)
A screen-printed fabric designed for St. Jude's. Angie's work
is not realist but her wonderful leaves and stems create stunning,
simple stylized shapes.

Bantie

www.bantie.se
info@bantie.se

10 //   Bantie is a design company based in Stockholm and run by Ulrika Gyllstad and Wilhelmina Wiese. Ulrika studied fashion design at Beckmans College of Design in Stockholm and she designs all of the printed fabrics at Bantie. The company is named after her Aunt Bantie who has always been a major source of inspiration. Bantie's vibrant print designs can be found on fabric, wallpaper, lamps, trays and much more.

Top / Salamander Rosamund
Every piece of this design is filled with interesting motifs and textures and was inspired by animal skins and lizards.

Bottom / Korall Bla
This striking linear print was inspired by the structure inside coral. Like all of Bantie's designs shown here it was first hand-drawn and then taken into Photoshop.

Opposite / Bubbel Pool Bla
A hand-drawn print which has been coloured and repeated in Photoshop. Inspired by bubbles in liquid, Ulrika wanted a graphic yet organic look for this fabric design.

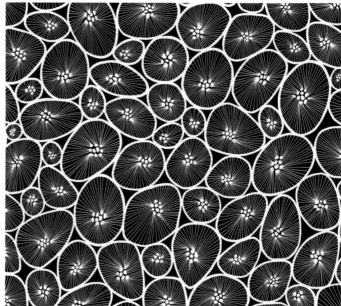

Beci Orpin

www.beciorpin.com
www.jackywinter.com
hello@beciorpin.com

11 //   Beci Orpin is based in Melbourne where she studied for a degree in Textile Design at RMIT. Beci has participated in over 30 exhibitions both locally and overseas (including five solo shows) and clients have included Burton Snowboards, Mercedes Benz, Built By Wendy, and Frankie Magazine. Beci says she feels very lucky every day to be doing a job that she loves and that never feels like work! In the future she sees herself designing for interiors – maybe some styling work too – as well as educational products and books for children.

Design Heroes:
Enzo Mari, Alexander Girard, Maurice Sendak, Bruno Munari, Lisa Larson.

Top / Folk Rabbit Journal
A journal design which forms part of Beci Orpin's own line of products sold in her shop and at stockists worldwide.

Bottom / Kit Cosmetic Bag
Part of a collaboration with Kit Cosmetics, for whom Beci designed the flagship store – exterior and interior – as well as cosmetic bags and a tote bag. She used Kit's signature colours to create something that was pop, super bold and colourful.

Top / Bird Portrait
with Flowers
Created using collaged paper
and gouache as an original
art piece from a series of
three. Beci often works with
silhouettes and paper collage
but this was the first time she
brought the two together.

Bottom / Year of the Ox
A Chinese New Year card
created in Adobe Illustrator
for Rebecca Wolkenstein to
send out to clients, featuring
a dark silhouette decorated
with bright embellishments.

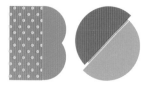

Belinda Strong

www.littlebeehive.com.au
www.honeyjumble.blogspot.com
bee@littlebeehive.com.au

12 // Belinda Strong lives in the beautiful Dandenong Ranges, east of Melbourne. She works as a freelance designer and is also represented by Bright Art Licensing. Belinda, who is also known as 'Bee', has always loved to draw, and from a very young age would spend hours getting creative with coloured pencils. Throughout her teenage years, she trained full-time to be a ballet dancer. However, her passion for dance subsided and at eighteen Bee went to university and studied metal-smithing for three years. She went on to work as a jeweller for a couple of years but then realized that her greatest joy was in fact illustrating and she decided to pursue this career path.

Design Heroes:
Grant Featherston, Mary Quant, Eyvind Earle, Verner Panton, Charlie Harper, Mary Blair.

Top / Mr Fox's New Hat
A limited edition art print created for Bee's own Little Beehive label on Etsy. The fox has a mid-century look and interesting stripe detail.

Bottom / Nelly
A greeting card created for Little Beehive of a mod floral elephant – the pink is slightly offset.

Top / Teapots
Here Bee has used a more muted colour palette to create a stylish portfolio piece. Notice how the shapes of the items fit together so beautifully.

Bottom / Fox's Morning Walk
Created as a portfolio piece this design features a friendly fox in striking orange, set against a pale grey ground.

Belly Button
Designs

www.bellybuttondesigns.com
www.bellybuttonblog.com
rachel@bellybuttondesigns.com

13 // Rachel Hare is the art director behind Belly Button Designs. Established in 1994 it is an independent greeting card design and publishing business. Rachel is from Manchester, but studied for a degree in Drawing and Painting at the Edinburgh College of Art, and a master's in Fine Art at the University of Ulster. At Belly Button the focus is on design and quality, and designs are often hand-painted at first. The finished products are entirely made in England, handmade and hand-finished. Also in the Belly Button design team are Ruth Fletcher and Emily Hauck. Stockists include John Lewis, Selfridges, and many independent stores in the United Kingdom, United States, Australia and Canada. They also have their own retail shop in West Didsbury, Manchester.

Design Hero:
Vivienne Westwood.

Top / General Floral
A sweet and carefree floral design featuring blossoms scattered over pale pink stripes.

Opposite top / Fluffies
Striking colours, fabulous patterns and cute, loveable characters feature in the children's range Fluffies. It includes design-led birthday cards for boys and girls like these number cards.

Opposite middle & bottom /
Fluff Cards
Belly Button's Fluff range of cards combines stunning bright colours (often in neon) with sophisticated illustration and design. The background is textured with cross hatch or gingham and for motifs patterns are layered on patterns.

1 one

2 two

3 three

have a beautiful birthday

happy birthday

a little something for you on your birthday

you're on the move

new home

Opposite top left /
General Stripes
The formality of regular stripes
have been disregarded for a
dynamic stack of jaunty angled
bars filled with pleasing
patterns.

Opposite top right /
General Spots
By playing with the scale of
these dots and filling them
with an imaginative selection
of patterns this design is
elevated to something special.

Opposite bottom /
General Butterflies
The strong house style means
Belly Button's brand is easily
identified, as with this butterfly
card. These patterns aren't just
used for greeting cards, but on
mugs, notebooks, gift wrap
and promotional merchandise.

Above / Knickerbocker
The Knickerbocker card range
is what the company is best
known for. All the cards are
hand-finished with glitter
and gems which is applied
in their Manchester studio.
In this design a graceful
sweeping stem provides an
anchor for all the motifs.

By Graziela

www.bygraziela.com
info@bygraziela.com

14 // Graziela Preiser has worked as a successful creative director, graphic designer and illustrator since 1965. Now with her daughter Nina they have founded a company By Graziela to re-launch Graziela's original designs from the 1970s and produce them on kids' products, tableware and fabrics. Graziela is originally from Berlin but is now based in Hamburg and her designs were hugely popular in Germany in the 1970s. She is influenced and inspired by travelling, and her passion for all optical graphic designs from paper arts, children's toys, Japanese textiles, and vintage wrapping papers. Awards have included a gold medal by the German Art Director's Club in 1973.

Design Heroes:
Sonia Delaunay, David Hockney, Eileen Green, Le Corbusier, Matisse.

Top / Farm
Originally designed in 1977, a pattern inspired by a dream to live on a farm, it features a cheerful farmer's family and a menagerie of animals. Farm was used on several textile products, wallpaper and on crockery and has been re-issued today as a poster.

Bottom / Apples
Originally designed in 1971, this design was hugely successful when released in two colour combinations : orange-yellow and blue-green. Apart from selling thousands of bedding sets it also sold 30,000 tablecloths, 26,000 kitchen towels and over 10,000 napkins. The fabric was also available per metre on the roll and sold over 30,000 metres!

Above / Leaves
Originally designed in 1979 this pattern was applied onto
bedding sets. You can find the trademark Graziela heart in the
leaves. All Graziela's designs were originally hand-drawn but
have now been vectorized.

Overleaf / 1,2,3
Originally designed in 1972, this cheerful and bold design is
perfect for teaching children to count. The design was applied
to wallpaper, fabric, kids' clothes and crockery sets.

Carolina Melis

www.carolinamelis.com
caro@carolinamelis.com

15 // Carolina Melis is originally from Italy but has been living in the United Kingdom since 2000. She attended Central Saint Martins and is currently based in East London. Alongside her career as an illustrator, Caroline also works as an animation director. This year she won a commission to make a film about textile design in Sardinia called *Le Fiamme di Nule* ('The Flames of Nule' after the design used on the carpets woven in the town of Nule). For inspiration Carolina loves folk motifs and textiles, strong colours and contrasts and she is a great fan of patterns used in tapestries, particularly in black and white. Her clients have included MTV, Microsoft, IKEA, Tank Magazine, Vogue, BBC, Sony and LeSportSac.

Right / Zino Uno 2/5
A digital illustration which has obvious influences from folk design, this second design in the series reflects Carolina's fascination for tapestry as the lines echo the shapes often found in weaving.

Opposite / Zino Uno 1/5
The first of a series of cards for IKEA named Zino Uno released worldwide for their 2011 collection. A scrolling circle framework is used to anchor all the beautiful folkloric motifs in a captivating repeat.

Opposite / Spring Collection
Commissioned by Microsoft for engraved designs and digital wallpapers for their Zune digital media player, the brief was to capture the theme of Spring and tap into Carolina's love of folk design.

Above / Zino Uno 3/5
This third Zino design is informed by an interest in weaving and yet it looks highly contemporary.

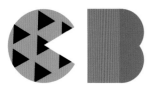

Caroline Bourlès

www.mytextiledesign.com
info@mytextiledesign.com

16 // My Textile Design is a creative studio specializing in pattern design, run by Caroline Bourlès. Caroline is from Brittany and studied textiles and graphic design in Paris. She creates prints for fashion, childrenswear, stationery and home design and has gained a lot of experience working for companies such as Erotokritos and Le Mont Saint Michel where she was responsible for trends analysis, colour research, fabrics choice and style drawings. Caroline has also designed for Victoria's Secret, Descamps, and Du Pareil Au Même.

Design Heroes:
Alain Gree, David Weidman, Takashi Iwasaki, Gemma Correll, Camilla Engman, Ana Montiel, Julia Wauters.

Above / Leaves
These decorative leaves in earthy autumnal colours are a great way of doing a floral motif without actually using flowers.

Opposite / Houses
Streets of houses with interesting architectural features are illustrated in outline only.

Overleaf left / Apples
Bold graphic apples of different sizes are arranged in a multi-directional layout. The triangle details add a contemporary touch.

Overleaf right / Fans
This organic pattern could also represent flowers, trees or leaves and is a lovely modern take on a classic theme.

Chamo

www.illustrissimo.fr
chamo.articho@yahoo.fr

17 // Chamo is currently based in Paris where she studied Textiles, followed by Illustration at the Duperré School of Applied Arts. After graduation she moved to Berlin to study Visual Communication and continued to illustrate, taking part in numerous exhibitions, both solo and collective. Five years later Chamo returned to Paris to work solely on illustration and is represented by the agency Illustrissimo. Projects have included CD covers, posters for plays and concerts, flyers, and editorial images for magazines. She has also produced several children's books, notably *ABCD Signes*, an alphabet book of sign-language, published by Thierry Magnier. In 2006, Chamo founded L'Articho, an association of artists and illustrators, which exhibits regularly in Paris.

Design Heroes:
Moolinex, John Broadley, Henning Wagenbreth, Jim Flora, Olle Eksell, Marcus Oakley, Benoit Jacques, 100% Orange.

Above / Poster Illustrissimo This Christmas 2009 poster has a wonderful retro feel thanks to the decorative font which is deliberately off register.

Bottom left / Abécédaire An alphabet poster where each letter is illustrated by a Chamo character. The wavy shaped border complements the light-hearted and playful drawing style.

Bottom right / Chamoland Extremely stylized birds, flowers and trees fill this forest. They may not be realistic but they are very expressive.

trissimo

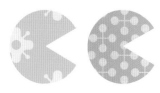

Cosmo Cricket

www.cosmocricket.com
eric@cosmocricket.com

18 // Cosmo Cricket is a paper crafting company created by married designers Julie and Eric Comstock. Based in Logan, Utah, they are renowned for their stylish and innovative scrapbook products. The couple met at the Utah State University in the Advertising Design program. They both went on to work in advertising as creatives for the next ten years. Inspiration for their work comes from diverse sources such as Charles and Ray Eames, Wilco, Eric's 9th grade art teacher, and their four children. Besides working on their own very successful label lines, clients have included EK Success, Andover Fabrics and Land of Nod.

Design Heroes:
Richard Dibenkorn, Mary Blair.

Right / Birds of a Feather
A paper sheet designed for all kinds of scrapbooking projects. Each bird is filled with detail and pattern for added depth against the muted red.

Opposite left / Birds Pattern
These pieces shows the birds working as individual elements and the wonderful variety of pattern fills available.

Opposite right /
Togetherness Chipboard Stickers
Eric and Julie wanted a vintage childhood feel that was fun and whimsical for these scrapbooking elements.

Ready-Set-Chip

19 PIECES | Togetherness™

©2010 Cosmo Cricket
Acid Free. Made in China
Togetherness RSC748

Cosmo Cricket

MADE WITH LOVE

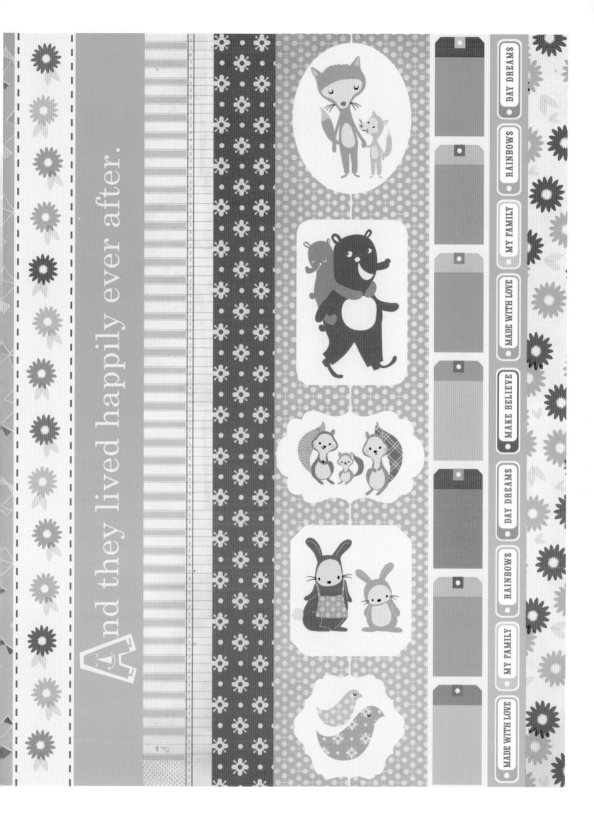

Opposite / Togetherness Elements
A sheet featuring tags and labels to cut out and use for paper crafting projects. The collection's theme was intended to celebrate all types of families and togetherness.

Above / Togetherness Borders
The design elements from the range are here arranged into stripes for creating borders and frames.

Darling Clementine

www.darlingclementine.no
post@darlingtime.no

19 //   Darling Clementine are Ingrid Reithaug and Tonje Holand, who run their company from Oslo. Together they publish their designs on greetings cards, gift wrap, tote bags, tea towels, notebooks and more. They also take on other design and illustration projects for clients, such as brand identity and children's T-shirt prints. Inspiration is drawn from a wide variety of sources, including flea markets and contemporary fashion.

Top / Marionette Cards
Among Darling Clementine's collections are the Marionettes – a set of characters in strikingly bold colours.

Bottom / Dog & Elephant
Two designs taken from the Claudettes card range – a series of fun animal designs with a vintage flavour.

Opposite / Toikka
Three designs from the Woodland collection – Home in the Hills, Florence the Fox and Peacock Tales. The designs are described as Scandinavian folk style but with a twist of modern.

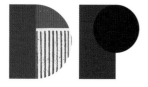

Debbie Powell

www.debbiepowell.net
www.dp-ink.blogspot.com
info@debbiepowell.net

20 // Debbie Powell is an illustrator, printmaker and hand-letterer originally from Bournemouth where she took a Fine Art diploma as well as a degree in Illustration at the Arts Institute. Now based in East London, Debbie has a love for texture and organic shapes. She uses all sorts of materials for creating her illustrations such as inks, paints, pen and pencil, stamps made from rubber and potatoes, silkscreen, lino cutting, paper cutting and Photoshop. Influences come from ancient jewellery, vintage textiles and all kinds of things, from seedpods to pottery, that Debbie comes across on her day to day travels. She also likes to document her inspirations on her blog. Clients have included Jamie Oliver, Marks & Spencer, Sparrow & Co, Simon & Schuster, and Walker Books. Debbie is represented by The Artworks in the UK and Mendola Art in the US.

Design Hero:
Saul Bass.

Top / Stems
Made from a cut paper pattern of simple stems all in one colour, with a texture applied in Photoshop.

Bottom / Flock of Birds
Hand-drawn with colours then applied in Photoshop. Debbie demonstrates that bird designs don't have to be whimsical.

Opposite / Footstool
Hand-drawn. Inspired by vintage furniture pieces, the footstools form a pattern and are themselves patterned, creating an almost abstract design.

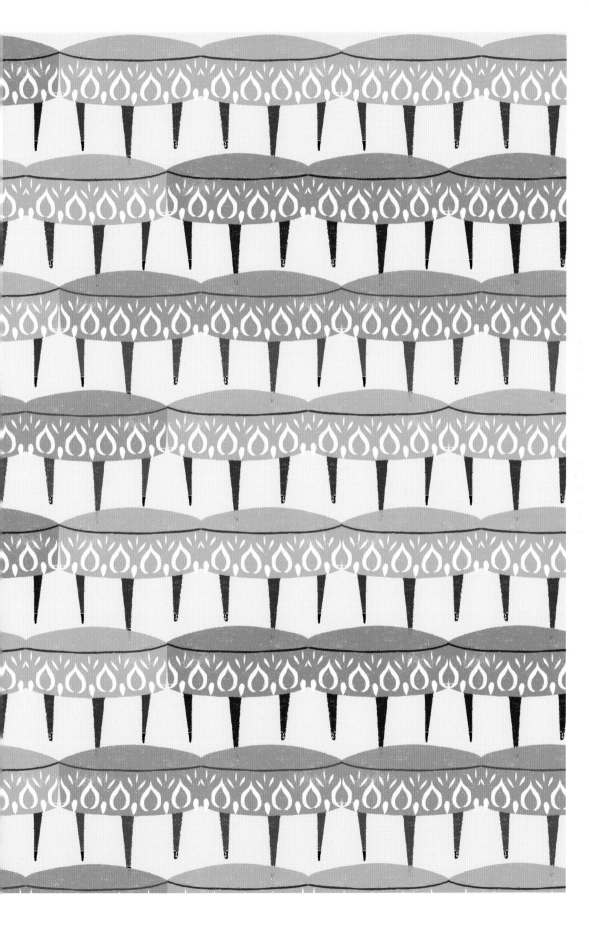

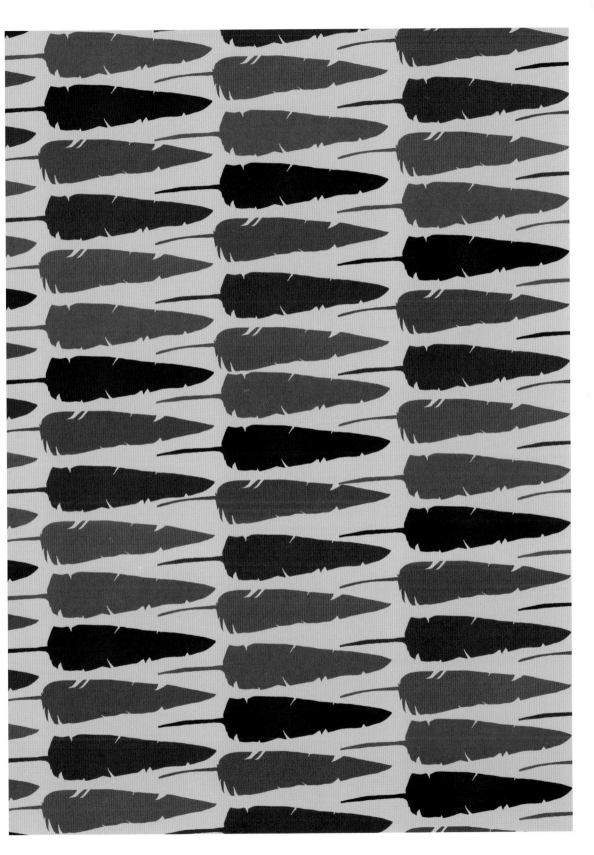

Opposite / Tea Cups
The dainty handles and graphic patterns on this hand-drawn piece were inspired by the teacups in Debbie's kitchen.

Above / Feathers
This screen-printed pattern features stylized feathers formally arranged in a stunning colour palette.

Dee Beale

www.deebeale.blogspot.com
www.deebeale.etsy.com

21 // Dee Beale is based in the Peak District, Derbyshire, UK where she creates her artwork for galleries and stores and for sale on Etsy. Dee studied Graphic Design and Illustration at North East Wales Institute Of Higher Education. She is a great fan of mid-century design and many of her design influences come from that era, along with a love for Scandinavian design and folk art. Dee has exhibited at The Royal Exchange Craft Shop in Manchester and the Affordable Art Fair in Battersea, London. She would now love to apply her designs to a range of fabrics and ceramics.

Design Hero:
Stig Lindberg.

Top / Winter Doves
Winter Doves was a design produced specifically for the festive season and like most of her prints started as work in her sketchbook. It is printed as a limited edition print on a Japanese Gocco in sparkly silver ink.

Bottom / Cornflowers
This design evolved from hand-drawn work in Dee's sketchbook which was then redrawn in Illustrator and then Gocco printed. Inspiration usually comes in the form of plant life and animals.

Top / White Anenomes
A stylized floral which was
informed by the graphic
but delicate nature of these
beautiful flowers.

Middle / Nordic Blue Hares
Inspired by photographs of
hares in a magazine, Dee
wanted a folk art style and
so mirrored the image and
added a floral pattern. It
is hand-printed using a
Japanese Gocco machine.

Bottom / Snowy Owl
Dee loves drawing birds and
finds the snowy owl especially
striking. Printed in orange
(as shown here) and silver
on a Japanese Gocco, it was
designed as a companion
piece to the Nordic Hares.

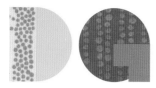

Designers Guild

www.designersguild.com
info@designersguild.com

22 //   Designers Guild was established in 1970 by Tricia Guild. They are renowned for their colourful, sumptuous collections of fabrics, wallpaper and home furnishings. From their store and showroom on the King's Road in London they have grown into one of the world's most highly acclaimed home furnishing manufacturers and are represented in over 60 countries worldwide. Never afraid to use bold, colourful or graphic patterns they also expanded into a complete line of bed and bath products, and developed licensing for stationery and fragrance. Tricia is also the author of many lifestyle books which explain her philosophies on interior design. Designers Guild have twice won the Queen's Award for Export Achievement and in 2008 Tricia Guild was awarded an OBE (Order of the British Empire) from the Queen for services to interior design.

Above / Central Park Lime
Fabric from the Manhattan Collection, 2009. Taking inspiration from the many types of tree found in Central Park this striking design is contemporary and graphic but with a sense of whimsy.

Opposite left / Ramblas Crocus
From the Barcelona Collection, 2010. Featuring stylistic roses that are brought alive by the contrast between the bright colours overprinted with black.

Opposite right / Ramblas Rose
From the Barcelona Collection, 2010. Designers Guild are renowned for their bold approach to florals and this ultra modern take on a traditional rose is no exception.

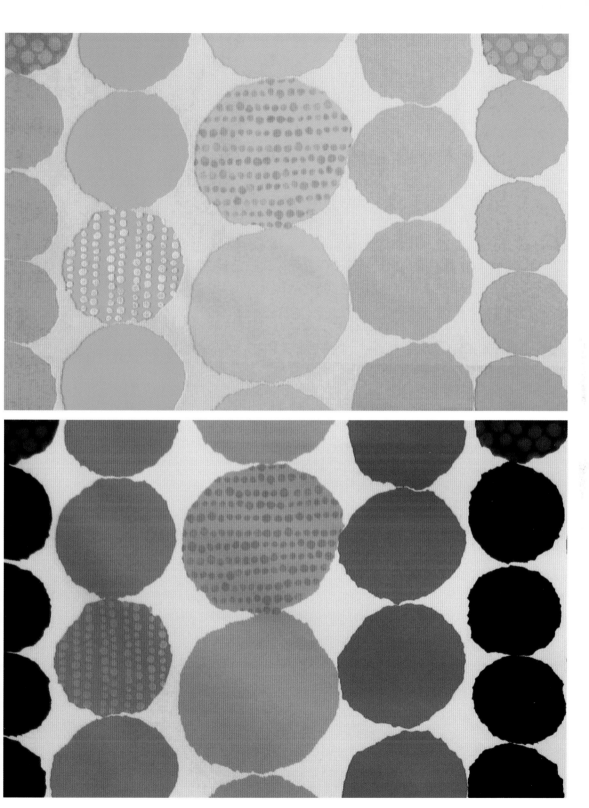

Opposite / Greenwich Village Turquoise
Fabric from the Manhattan Collection,
2009. The leaves of this design almost
form a geometric grid as they criss-cross
in horizontal and vertical directions.

Top / Tribeca Leaf
Fabric from the Manhattan Collection,
2009. The hand-painted nature of this
pattern has created beautifully irregular
shapes and a lovely sense of spontaneity.

Bottom / Tribeca Cerise
Fabric from the Manhattan Collection,
2009. Tricia Guild oversees the whole
creative process at Designers Guild and
her love of painting is evident.

Donna Wilson

www.donnawilson.com
info@donnawilson.com

23 // Donna Wilson is originally from Aberdeenshire in North East Scotland but now lives in London. She studied Textiles at Gray's School of Art in Aberdeen before gaining a master's degree in Mixed Media and Constructed Textiles at The Royal College of Art in London. It was during her time at the RCA that she began selling her knitted designs in top London store Couverture to great success. After graduation Donna set up her own studio and now employs several studio staff and knitters who work all around the United Kingdom. She is committed to making products that will last and her designs can be found on sale in 15 countries around the world, including stockists such as Heal's, John Lewis and Liberty.

Top / Robin Cushion
Knitted in Scotland, this cute bird design will stand the test of time thanks to its simplicity.

Bottom /
House Shaped Cushion
A whimsical design that evokes nostalgia with its simplicity and retro colouring. Photograph by Gareth Hacker.

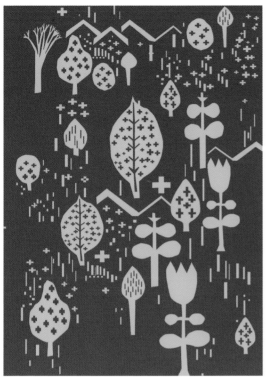

Top left / Leaves & Twigs
A scattered print design that is available on cushions made
from 100% cotton printed in the UK.

*Top righ*t / Mountain Spot
This beautiful pattern in shades of blue and turquoise was
designed with a rug in mind.

Bottom left / Owl Beaker
A colourful bright owl design which is handmade and printed
in Stoke-on-Trent, England. Photograph by Gareth Hacker.

Bottom right / Bird's Nest Plate
A stylized frame of sticks sets off the simplicity of the bird
in this ceramic design. Photograph by Gareth Hacker.

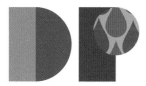

Draw! Pilgrim

www.drawpilgrim.com
drawpilgrim@gmail.com

24 // Pilgrim Lee is from Adelaide where she studied Visual Communication at the University of South Australia. Now based in Melbourne, Pilgrim works as a freelance designer for clients such as Modern Kiddo, I Heart Guitar and Kitschy Digitals. She grew up surrounded by art and design books in her mother's graphic design studio and, from a really early age, she had definite ideas about style. She is inspired by 1960s and '70s design and the colourful bold and beautiful aspects of those decades are reflected in her work.

Design Heroes:
Maija Isola, Alexander Girard, John Clappison, Georges Briard, Vera Neumann.

All / D, F, G, K, N, S :
The alphabet series is a collection of 26 prints based on the letters of the alphabet. Some are literal connections between letter and object (e.g. 'R' is for 'Rabbit') and some are more abstract, but all experiment with the combination of shape, colour and negative space. Pilgrim's inspirations were the sleek, futuristic forms and colours of Verner Panton and Arne Jacobsen amongst others. All of the designs were created in Adobe Illustrator as a personal project.

Dwell Studio

www.dwellstudio.com
customerservice@dwellstudio.com

25 //   Dwell Home Furnishings was founded in 1999 by Christiane Lemieux to design bedding for various clients such as Crate & Barrel and Bed, Bath & Beyond. After several years she decided to focus on designing for her own brand as she longed to have complete creative control. And so in 2005 Dwell Studio was born and began to produce its own beautiful high-end bedding to sell to design-led speciality stores. This was a great success and even led the studio to sign a deal to create a line exclusively for Target. Christiane now owns the company with her husband, Joshua Young, and they are assisted by partner Jennifer Chused. Their design inspiration comes from everywhere, be it from old fabrics and wallpaper, books, fashion or architecture. In 2010 they opened their first store in Manhattan within ABC Carpet & Home and their aim is to offer furniture and design for every room in a home.

Design Heroes:
Consuelo Castiglioni from Marni, Alan Campbell, Miuccia Prada, Dries Van Noten.

Top / Motif
Simple graphic motifs that are boldly rendered reinforce Dwell Studio's refreshing approach to designing for children.

Bottom / Gio Aqua
Dwell Studio's designs for babies and children feature prints that are crisp and stylish. They have brought a modern aesthetic to nursery prints and breathed new life into the standard children's theme of animals.

Opposite / Garden
A stylized floral pattern created for nursery bedding and accessories. The colour palette is surprisingly sophisticated for children's design and was ahead of its time. The effect is a pleasing folky pattern that is soft and appealing but, despite being designed for little girls, refuses to be cutesy.

Edholm Ullenius

www.edholmullenius.se

26 // Sissi Edholm and Lisa Ullenius are based in Stockholm where they both studied at Beckmans College of Design. Upon graduating they received a scholarship from IKEA and their company Edholm Ullenius was born. Since then they have designed for Paul Smith, Absolut Vodka, IKEA and the Museum of Modern Art, among others. Inspiration comes largely from nature and animals. Their dream commission would be to design the exteriors of a tall building – something really big!

Design Heroes:
Lucienne Day, Stig Lindberg, Saul Bass, Dan Wolgers.

Top / Bärbar
Designed as a tray for IKEA. This eye-catching and bright bird design turned out to be a bestseller!

Bottom /
Svabba Dishcloths/Aprons/ Soft Soap Bottle
Part of a collection for IKEA's cleaning products. Their brief was to turn cleaning into something joyful and these colourful apron designs certainly do the trick. The retro style floral motif follows through onto dishcloths and even a soap bottle.

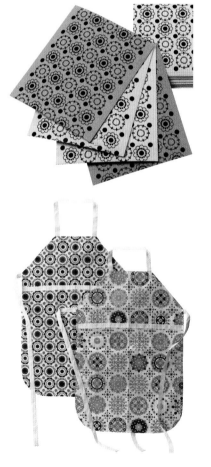

Top / Flower
Rows of flowers made from hearts were created for a card made for Bookbinders Design.

Bottom / Amaranten
This textured black and white pattern is part of a graphic identity designed for the restaurant Amaranten in Stockholm where it appeared on the menus. After a while, all the menus were stolen, and according to the staff it was because of the desirable design.

EG

Eleanor Grosch

www.justeleanor.com
www.justeleanor.com/blog
eleanor@justeleanor.com

27 //   Eleanor Grosch grew up in Largo, Florida but is now based in Philadelphia. She studied Fine Art at the University of South Florida and now works as a commercial illustrator. Eleanor is known for her stylized animal and bird designs which use graphic lines and forms to show the essence of their shape. Her inspirations mainly come from modernist design and illustration, cute animals, skateboard and poster art. Clients have included Keds, Urban Outfitters, Westminster Fabrics, Giro, Alien Workshop, SNIFTY, Wilco, and the Dave Matthews Band. Eleanor also designs her own line of products and creates screen-prints of her popular works. She would love to design wallpaper in the future.

Design Heroes:
Ben Shahn, Miró, Charley Harper, Alexander Girard, Chagall.

Top / Forest
Smooth arcs and stylized shapes fit together beautifully in this animal print, created for Eleanor's own stationery line.

Bottom / Zoo 2
Fun colours and a playfully arranged assortment of animals, created as a fabric print released by Westminster Fabrics.

Opposite / Chickadee
For this print Eleanor has simplified the birds down to the basic elements and designed a repeat that has an almost optical effect. Created for Urban Outfitters.

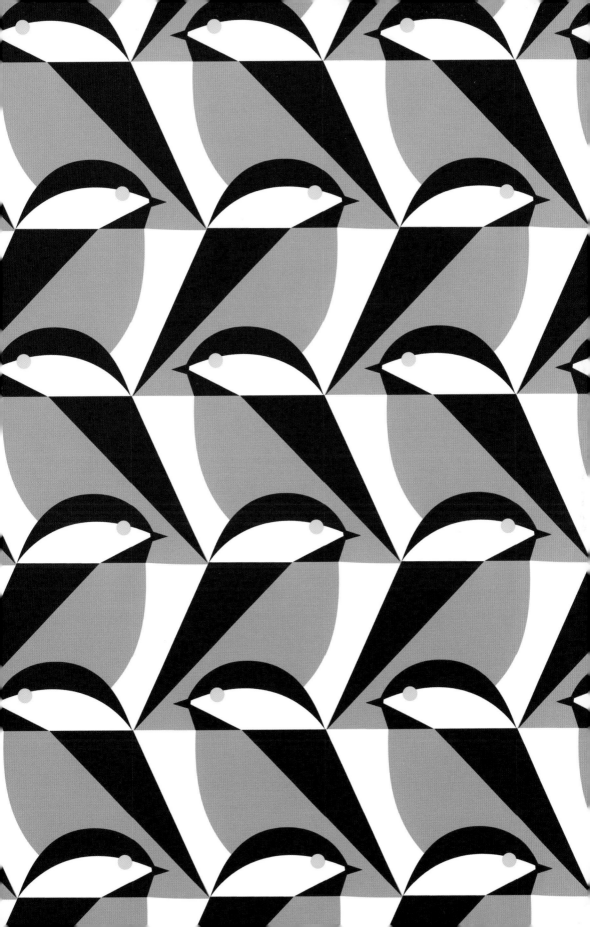

Opposite / Veggies
This traditional kitchen print is given a modern makeover by
Eleanor on this proposed design for Joseph Joseph.

Above / Aviary
Clever use of colour and the dense coverage of the pattern make
this design really striking. Created as a proposed design for
Westminster Fabrics.

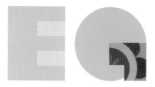

Ellen Giggenbach

www.elleng.co.nz
www.ellengiggenbach.blogspot.com
ellengiggenbach@xtra.co.nz

28 // Ellen Giggenbach was born in Bavaria in Germany but now lives in Wellington, New Zealand. Ellen first studied Graphic Art in Vienna and then took her diploma in New Zealand. Her inspiration and passion comes from a love of European folk art and the quirky and sometimes kitsch designs and colours of the 1950s and '60s. She obsessively collects games, record covers, children's books, fabric and china from this era. Ellen begins each piece by cutting, placing, moving and often exchanging a series of graphic shapes, which are carefully cut from art paper that she has previously painted with acrylics in a large selection of beautiful colours. Clients have included Air New Zealand, Lantern Studios, Galison and Calypso Cards.

Design Heroes:
Orla Kiely, Tricia Guild.

Top / Kitchen Maid
Each design starts its life as a mere idea and piece by piece it grows like a puzzle until the point when just one more element would upset a carefully composed balance of shape and colour.

Bottom / Autumn Pear & Summer Orange
These stylized fruits were hand-cut and made from assembled paper, as part of a series of woodblock mounted prints. The shapes are very simple and graphic to give the colours maximum impact.

Top / Festive Fare
Created for kitchen tablewares
and stationery, this design
was inspired by mid-century
cookbook illustrations and
made using hand-cut and
assembled paper for Lantern
Studios.

Bottom / Festive Bird &
Festive Butterfly
Created as a set of wall
decals for Chocovenyl these
bold motifs were inspired
by Mexican folk art.

Left / Love Birds
Ellen's original pieces were
hand-cut and assembled in
paper and then repeated in
Photoshop. The single motif
was used on a greeting card
with the repeat on gift wrap.

Top / Pretty Bird
Part of a range of stationery
and household products for
Lantern Studios. The design
was deliberately divided into
sections where each piece
could be used separately or
as a whole.

Bottom / Bouquet
Hand-cut from assembled
paper as a greeting card for
Lagom Design this was
inspired by mid-century
wallpaper motifs.

Fiona Howard

www.fionahoward.com
www.fifibyfionahoward.com
fihoward@mac.com

29 // Brighton-based designer Fiona Howard has over 20 years experience in the design industry, working for clients such as IKEA, Habitat, John Lewis and Marks & Spencer. Fiona also created the classic and popular Clocks design for Sanderson (see page 276). During her career she has designed textiles, greeting cards and wall art. Besides a successful freelance career she also has her own label, Fifi, producing her own collection of fabrics and products.

Top / Angelica Fabric
Fiona uses hand-cut lino to create her fabric prints. This one shows her skill in stylizing natural forms.

Middle / Angelica and Hydrangea
A pair of cushions from Fiona's own label, for which she creates a variety of products using her textile designs. The coastal blues reflect her seaside living, and the deep pink is taken from nature's flowers.

Bottom / Fifi Mugs
Produced by MS Mugs, Fiona's collections are sold in some of the UK's most stylish shops. The designs use a muted palette inspired by nature with stylized leaves and birds.

Opposite / Fifi Beach Hut
An overall view of this collection shows how Fiona has cleverly created a palette and prints that work perfectly together.

Frances Moran

www.pocoprint.com.au
studio@pocoprint.com.au

30 // Frances Moran is from Melbourne where she studied for a degree in Fine Art Printmaking at Victoria College, and another degree in Textile Design at RMIT University. Frances has worked as a designer both in-house and freelance on projects for bedding, furnishing fabrics, cushions, rugs, accessories, childrenswear, stationery, cards, wrapping paper and packaging. She finds inspiration in children's books, Scandinavian design, vintage wallpaper, retro fabrics and ceramics, design books and animations from the 1960s and '70s. Frances says her design style can vary enormously but her work for Poco Print is largely composed of cute, simple, graphic patterns. She likes being her own boss and working all hours from her home studio. Her dream commission would be to do a fabric range for IKEA.

Design Heroes:
Marimekko, Florence Broadhurst, Lucienne Day, Charley Harper, Dick Bruna.

Above / Emmeline
A retro-inspired decorative geometric flower/petal pattern. Designed for Alluminare for their custom product range.

Opposite / Bonnie Tree
A stylized graphic tree pattern created in Illustrator. Designed for Alluminare for custom lampshades, fabric, cushions and wallpaper.

Future Shelter

www.futureshelter.com
www.futureshelter.blogspot.com

31 // Jane King set up Little Design Horse, a textile and surface pattern studio, in 2005. It had clients worldwide and proved very successful but all the work it produced was done 'anonymously' behind the scenes for bigger brands. And so Future Shelter was set up in 2008 so that the studio could concentrate on designing its own range of products which it could then print itself. Jane is originally from the United Kingdom and studied for a degree in Printed Textile Design at Loughborough College of Art and a master's degree in Printed Textiles at the Royal College of Art. She is now based in Perth, Australia, however. All the designs featured here are by Jane except for Park which is by her sister Liz King. Jane says of Future Shelter 'We have total control and don't have to follow any trends – we create whatever we feel like that day!' Her aim is to do more designs for lighting, furniture and ceramics.

Design Heroes:
Lucienne Day, Stig Lindberg.

Top / Retrodot
Created as a fun geometric floral, Retrodot was originally designed as a canvas but then developed into coasters.

Bottom / Park
Designed by Liz King for Future Shelter this design has a magical and colourful park landscape full of stylized trees.

Top left / Papercut Garden
Created as an all-over print
for cushions and lampshades
this was hand-drawn in a
sketchbook, scanned and put
into repeat using Illustrator. It
was inspired by the Botanical
Gardens in King's Park, Perth,
and the art of paper cutting.

Top right / Elephant/Pear
Created first for T-shirts and
later developed into brooches,
these were designed in
Illustrator and laser-cut in
their studio. The inspiration
came from modern lace.

Bottom / Lemon Fish
This was designed for a tea
towel and drawn with inks on
watercolour paper, then
scanned and developed
in Illustrator before being
screen-printed on linen or
cotton. It was inspired by her
retro ceramic collection and
their own lemon tree.

Gillian Blease

www.gillianblease.co.uk
mail@gillianblease.co.uk

32 // Gillian Blease is currently based in South East London. She studied Fine Art and is principally an editorial illustrator but a particularly decorative series of illustrations created for a recipe column in *The Guardian* led to a commission for tablemats from Jenny Duff. Further patterns requests soon followed. Her clients have included John Lewis, Random House and Rockport Publishers who published a book of Gillian's patterns in 2009 called *Pattern and Palette 3*. Her inspiration comes mostly from the 'everyday' and looking around, but also from observing labels, signs, logos, visiting the Victoria and Albert Museum and folk art. Gillian's patterns are available for licensing from The Bright Agency. One of her ambitions is to branch out into the greeting card market.

Design Heroes:
Josef Frank, Walter Allner, Edward Bawden, Mary Fedden.

Top / Back to Front Circle
A design created for gift wrap featuring a geometric pattern of intersecting circles in a superb palette of pinks, reds and purples.

Bottom / Diamond Star
Demonstrating Gillian's wonderful skill with geometric shapes, this gift wrap design could be floral or stars and the hot colours are balanced by cool grey.

Opposite / Fig Slice
Created for the 'Sugar and Spice' chapter in Gillian's *Pattern and Palette 3* book, simplified shapes of figs filled with seeds are arranged in a two directional pattern.

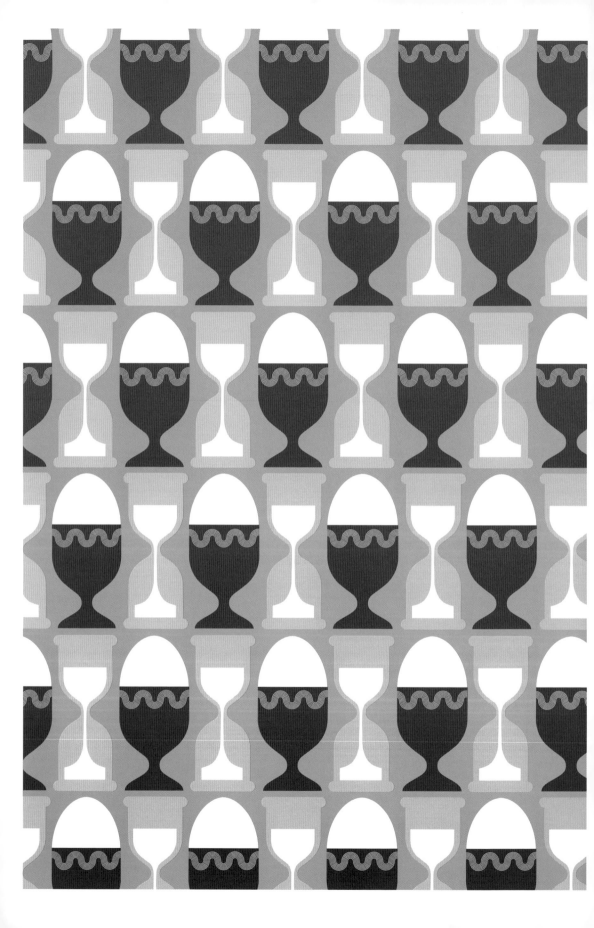

Opposite / Eggs For Tea
One of a set of six food-related designs for Jenny Duff
tableware. Ogee shaped egg timers and stylized egg cups form
a very fluid pattern.

Above / A Squeeze of Lemon
One of a set of six food-related designs created for Jenny Duff
tableware. Gillian has beautifully stylized a lemon squeezer
and arranged an orderly repeat, with some left empty and others
containing a lemon.

Graphic Nothing

www.graphicnothing.com
www.someprints.com
hello@graphicnothing.com

33 // Gary Clarke grew up in Leicester but is now based at his kitchen table in South Manchester. He has spent most of his career designing for the music industry creating websites and record sleeves for bands such as Portishead and Badly Drawn Boy. Gary describes himself as 'rather like Hong Kong Phooey – I have a mild-mannered boring daytime job and secret evenings of being Graphic Nothing.' His graphic designs have received almost a million views on the Flickr website and have now been made available as prints. Inspiration comes from many places including an obsession with the golden ratio 61.8% found in nature and architecture – many of his pattern experiments come from this. He thinks it would be fun to see some of his work end up as wallpaper in people's homes, so that could be the next step for him.

Design Hero:
Andy Votel.

Top /
Garden of Spiky Delights
Sharp angles and striking use of opacity make this design inspired by the game Kerplunk really stand out.

Bottom /
Geometric Pattern 27
Experiments with circles and CMYK colour makes for a bold pop art pattern.

Opposite top left /
Place de Clichy
Gary creates all of his designs in Illustrator and says 'They all repeat, but it's not easy to see where they do.'

Opposite top right /
Montparnasse
This work is typical of Gary's experiments in trying to make the 'visual equivalent of melodic harmonies with colour and shape.'

Opposite bottom /
L'urbanisme
Curved half circles contrast with the hard lines of triangles in this superbly designed geometric print.

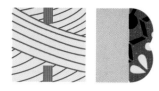

Hillary Bird

www.hillarybird.com
www.etsy.com/shop/hillarybird
hillarybirdshop@gmail.com

34 // Hillary Bird grew up in the rolling hills of Virginia – which she thinks explains her fixation for illustrating animals – but she is now based in San Francisco. Although Hillary lives on the West Coast, she says she will always be an East Coast girl at heart. She studied for a degree in Textiles from the Rhode Island School of Design in Providence – where she actually started out in architecture until she realized she liked fabric and pattern more! Hillary is constantly inspired by vintage fabric, wallpaper, mid-century style, animals, knitting, flea markets, Swedish design, and 'the absurd'. She finds inspiration can come from the most unexpected place – a graffiti tag, a piece of trash – as long as her eyes are open to it.

Design Heroes:
Yoshitomo Nara, Hella Jongerius, Prada, Charles and Ray Eames.

Above / Colt Love
Hillary likes to sketch out all her illustrations first by hand to help get a sense of layout, line weight and texture. She then scans them into the computer to digitally colour them and adjust as needed.

Opposite top / Squirrel Jam
Textured squirrel characters are perfectly set off by the striking frame design and bold colours.

Opposite bottom left /
In Cahoots
This pattern reduces the owl into an almost geometric shape to create a strong repeat design.

Opposite bottom right /
Fairisle Fox
For this design, Hillary's inspiration came from knitting patterns.

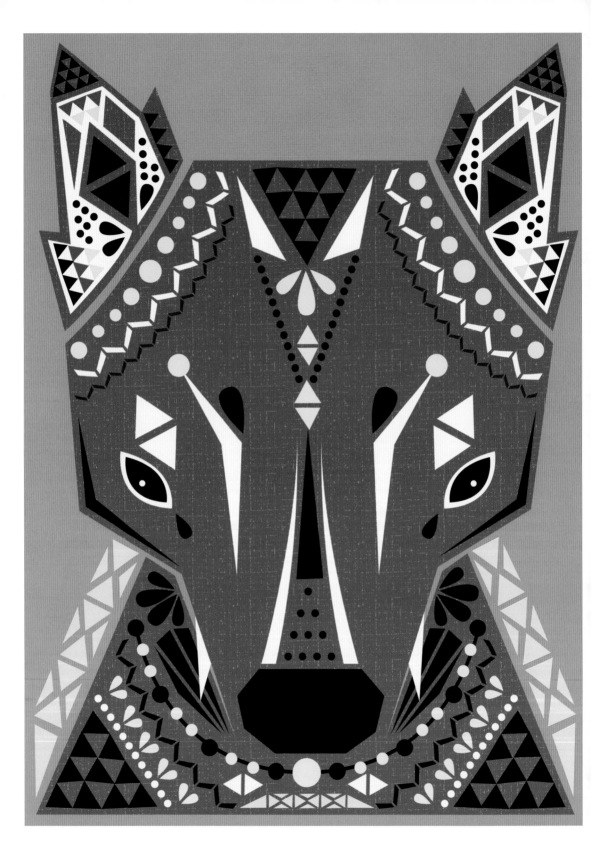

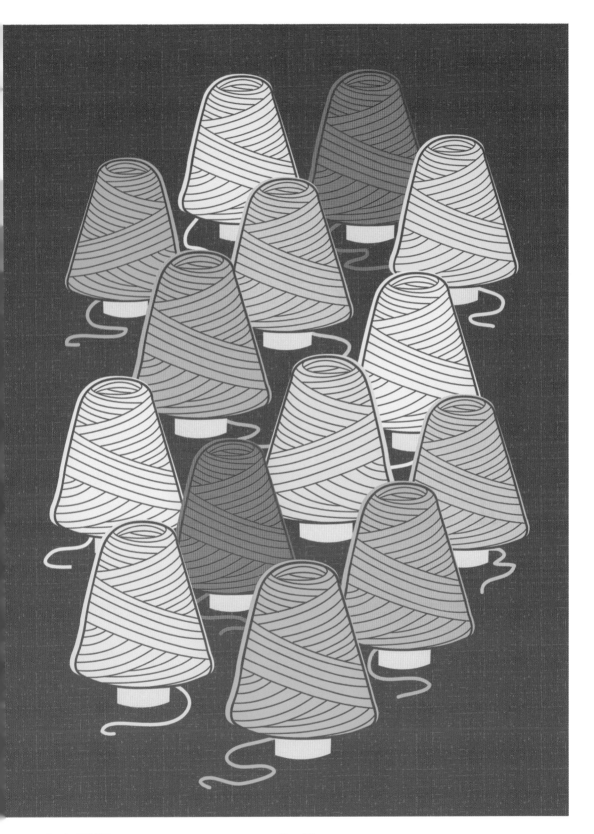

Opposite / Wolf King
Angular geometric shapes are used to create the form of the
wolf and to decorate it all over with dramatic results.

Above / Yarntown
To make her art prints to sell on Etsy, Hillary prints her work
using archival pigment ink on archival fine art paper, as in this
sewing design where the dark base really highlights the
coloured spools of thread.

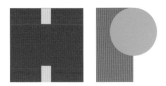

Hsinping Pan

www.hsinpingpan.com
www.lillarogers.com
hsinping@gmail.com

35 // Hsinping Pan was born in Taiwan but spent 11 years living and working in Los Angeles where she studied for a master's degree in Animation at the University of Southern California. Now back in Taipei, Hsinping works as a freelance designer and is represented by Lilla Rogers for her illustration work. Her influences come largely from children's books – in which she loves colour and simple shapes – and Hsinping also likes to put small stories into her designs. Clients have included Oopsy Daisy, Peaceable Kingdom Press, and Magic Murals. She would very much like to work in book design.

Design Heroes:
Saul Bass, Paul Rand, Sara Fanelli.

Top /
Elephant & The Boy
Hsinping used a mixture of digital design with hand-drawn texture on this cover art for *Babybug* magazine.

Bottom / Letter Lion
Created in Illustrator using hand-drawn texture, this formed part of a fun and cheerful animal alphabet piece.

Opposite top /
Hot Balloon Trip
A personal drawing which again uses the medium of Illustrator with hand-drawn texture.

Opposite bottom /
It's A Big World
Drawn with acrylic then composited on a computer this is one image from a music video Hsinping made for a song called 'It's a Big World' by Renee and Jeremy.

35 / Hsinping Pan

Opposite / 3 Flowers
Created in Illustrator for a fabric for Australian children's
clothing company Three Little Trees.

Above / Fireworks & The Bird
Another fabric created for Three Little Trees, this fun design
uses a riot of colours.

Ian Bilbey

www. ianbilbey.com
www.centralillustration.com

36 //   London based illustrator
Ian Bilbey studied Graphic Design
at the Royal College of Art. After
graduating he went to work at
Pentagram, and now works as a
freelance designer and illustrator.
Ian has enjoyed a long working
relationship with Paul Smith
creating products, graphics and
clothing. Other clients have
included *Wallpaper* magazine,
Penguin Books, Sir Terence Conran
and The Royal Mail.

Design Heroes:
Richard Scarry, Colin Chapman,
Joan Miró.

Top / ABC
Created for *FX* magazine,
Ian used a mouse to draw
these highly decorative blocks.

Bottom left /
Paul Smith – Valentine
A brief was given to Ian
to illustrate Valentine's Day
shopping at Paul Smith.
Although at first it may look
feminine and romantic a
closer look reveals masculine
motifs such as a helicopter,
racing car and speedboat.

Bottom right / Going Dutch
An editorial piece on Holland
in *FX* magazine led Ian to
create a Dutch folk-inspired
design that has strong clean
lines.

Opposite /
Restaurant Magazine
A beautifully decorated cake
piled high with pattern on an
ornate trolley was featured on
the front cover of a restaurant
magazine.

Inaluxe

www.inaluxe.blogspot.com
www.inaluxe.bigcartel.com
inaluxe@iinet.net.au

37 //   Inaluxe are Kristina Sostarko and Jason Odd from Melbourne. They have completely different reference points and styles, but working on both collaborative and individual work under the Inaluxe name keeps everything fresh and exciting. When asked what inspires her work Kristina says, 'The desire to exceed expectations and create new experiences. That's the driving force to creating, but the inspiration comes from all over the place.' In a more tangible way, inspiration comes from obscure surf, mod, jazz and soul music, alternative cinema, books, mid-century modern architecture, spaghetti westerns, velvet furniture, and a list so long it would take them years to complete. Recent projects have included designing for Blue Q products and they are currently working on a range of textile prints.

Design Heroes:
Christian Dior, Mark Rothko, Andy Warhol, Robert Rauschenberg.

Above / Sliced Au
Go Go – Au Naturelle
Collage and gouache on paper.
Inspired by the 1960s, this design
is filled with interesting textures.

Opposite / Orbital
Gouache and colouring pen
on paper. This forms part of
the Inaluxe pattern series and
consists of sliced circles on a
linen-look base.

Opposite top / Helsinki Afternoon August 1969 Gouache on paper. The first Inaluxe design to make it into *giclée* print format, it features a bold rendition of stylized trees.

Opposite bottom / One Million Short Stories Gouache and ink on paper designed for *giclée* print. The cross hatched texture makes an effective background for these colourful shapes that reference apostrophes.

Above / The Speculators Gouache on paper. Part of their birds series, this piece shows another side of Inaluxe's work as they are fabulous at creating whimsical creatures. The balance is perfect between the use of graphic shapes and muted colours.

Ingela P. Arrhenius

www.ingelaparrhenius.com
www.soderbergagentur.com
hello@ingelaparrhenius.com

38 // Ingela P. Arrhenius was born in Holland – to a Swedish father and a German mother – but her family moved to Sweden when she was two years old. Ingela studied Graphic Design at Berghs School of Communication in Stockholm, and now lives just outside the city in Enskede working as a freelance illustrator. She has designed many wonderful things including stamps for the Swedish Post, children's clothes for Kapp Ahl, patterns for Bookbinders Design, cards for Lagom Design, and posters for OMM Design. Ingela has also produced a lot of illustrations for advertising and packaging over the years. She says the biggest inspiration for her work comes from old children's books which she finds at flea markets.

Design Heroes:
Olle Eksell, Stig Lindberg,
Åke Lewerth.

Top / Roundels
The bolder the better for this pictorial geometric created as a personal project for an exhibition at Designgalleriet, Stockholm.

Bottom / Birthday Elephant
Created as a greeting card for Lagom Design, for whom Ingela has designed quite a few ranges. The aim was to capture a certain playfulness.

Top left / My Kitchen Shelves
A fabulous selection of typically Scandinavian kitchenalia have been beautifully illustrated using the shelving as a layout device to hold it all together. A personal project for a limited edition tea towel.

Top right / Tea Towel
The narrow line detailing on the various foods soften the flat graphics and add interest to this personal project for a limited edition tea towel.

Bottom left / Tree
Created as a greetings card for Lagom Design and a poster for OMM Design, it features a crisp graphic tree that is jam packed with Ingela's wonderful characters.

Bottom right / Winter Tree
From part of Ingela's stunning 2010 Christmas card range for Lagom Design. The bright acid colours contrast against the pale blue and make a refreshing approach to festive design.

Opposite / A–Z Lotto Game
Ingela had tremendous fun working on these A–Z illustrations
for a personal project. In between jobs she would use them to
play around with various colour combinations. They were
designed for possible use on posters or perhaps a memory game.

Above / Bird In Tree
Birds, bees and a jolly sun look striking in red, white and blue
on this card created for UNICEF.

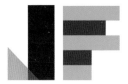

Jane Foster

www.janefoster.co.uk
www.janefosterblog.blogspot.com
jane@janefoster.co.uk

39 // Jane Foster is originally from Essex but is now based in Devon. She is a self-taught artist who works with screen-printing and vintage fabrics which she sells through her own website as well as galleries. Her clients have included Habitat, Clothkits and The Art Group, with whom she has published several card ranges as well as art prints. Jane's work is strongly influenced by 1950s and '60s Scandinavian design and she has a passion for collecting vintage ceramics, Formica, books and prints. She would love to design fabrics, storage jars, trays and tins for a company such as Marimekko.

Design Heroes:
Lucienne Day, Marianne Westman, Orla Kiely.

Top / Dove Games
Jane's screen-prints all start off as ink drawings. This one comprises two fabulously detailed yet delicate birds.

Middle / Stockholm
Screen-printed onto fabrics, this retro geometric design has wonderful crisp clean lines, whose squares are softened by adding a slight bulge.

Bottom left / Scandinavian Flower Cards
A collection of greeting cards for The Art Group featuring Jane's striking flower drawings where she plays with colour and scale to make each one unique.

Bottom right / Happy Animal Cards
Jane has incorporated her wonderful vintage fabric collection into this range of print/collage cards for The Art Group.

Opposite / Atomic Fish
This striking one colour screen-print design for paper beautifully displays a 1950s Festival of Britain influence but still looks modern and original.

Jane Mosse

www.janemosse.co.uk
jane@janemosse.co.uk

40 // Jane Mosse trained as a textile designer at Trent Polytechnic in Nottingham and went on to work at Dorma for two years. In 1986 she established her own business working freelance and alone at first, but she now has a team of highly creative designers under her direction. The studio's expertise and emphasis on quality and colour mean that it is one of the most up-to-date and dynamic companies of its kind. Jane believes that the success of her studio comes from creating images that easily translate into a variety of products from stationery and gifts to bedlinen and furnishing fabrics. Their client list is extensive and designs are either supplied from the portfolio or commissioned from across Europe, America and Asia. Jane regularly exhibits at Heimtextil in Germany and Surtex in New York. The studio is based in the grounds of a sixteenth century farmhouse in Hampshire, where Jane is inspired by her two children and her beautiful garden.

Above / Birds In Trees
By Rachel Hatchard
A hand-painted design in a pretty ice cream palette, Rachel also created a bespoke version of the design for her own son's bedroom.

Opposite top left / Butterflies
By Ann Johnstone
Graphic butterflies in stark black and white are interspersed with brightly coloured ones in this striking pattern inspired by a visit to a butterfly garden.

Opposite top right / Folk Design
By Nidhi vij Kapur
Folkloric motifs are boldly rendered and arranged in a box layout.

Opposite bottom left / Alphabet
By Ingrid Goode
Decorative letters are filled with a variety of spots and checks to create a fun design that is full of detail.

Opposite bottom right / Bright Owls
By Hannah Sessions
A quirky hand-drawn style gives these owls a childlike appeal.

Opposite / Tweed Cows
By Wendy MacFarlane
Friendly-looking cows are cleverly filled with simple and
complex patterns.

Above / Floral Wiggly Trees
By Lesley Liddiard
A delicate arrangement of trees and blossoms repeat beautifully
thanks to their organic waving shapes.

Jane Ormes

www.janeormes.co.uk
www.figshop.co.uk
janeormes@blueyonder.co.uk

41 // Jane Ormes studied Printed Surface Design at Leicester Polytechnic and currently lives and works in Bristol where she concentrates on creating limited edition silkscreen prints. Having worked for greeting card companies for many years screen-printing gave Jane an opportunity to create images just for herself. She had just moved into a new house that was full of blank walls and the first couple of years were spent creating prints just to decorate the house. She now sells her work in galleries and through her own website. Clients have included Paperlink, Dorling Kindersley and Greenpeace.

Design Heroes:
Orla Kiely, Brian Wildsmith, Dick Bruna, Eric Carle, Charley Harper.

Top / British Bird Unaware He'd Flown To Australia
Jane says, 'I love pattern and it always works its way into a design.'

Bottom / Cat With A Fish On Its Mind
Jane really loves fresh clear images that hark back to vintage posters and children's illustrations from the 1950s and '60s, so some of her work has a distinctly retro feel.

Opposite top / Mr Delmonte He Say Again 'Oi Get Off My Trees'
Inspiration can often come from an absurd or whimsical notion that pops up in Jane's head. The trees are full of detail and the palette features stylish greens and greys.

Opposite bottom left / Birds Nest In Blue
A simplified design that uses texture and pattern with great delicacy.

Opposite bottom right /
Shake A Tail Feather Baby
What could have been a simple design is given interest by a terrific use of textures.

17/70   shake a tail feather baby   Jane Ormes 2010

41 / Jane Ormes

Opposite / 2 Go Mad In Dorset
Using hand-printed silkscreens each colour is printed separately
and the image is built up layer by layer. These rabbits were also
featured in Jane's range of greeting cards for The Art Press.

Above / Semi Detached Housemartins
Inspired by a stay on a farm in North Devon where she saw
housemartins swooping, in this design most of the movement is
cleverly provided by the stems and grasses.

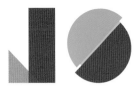

Jen Skelley

www.jenskelley.com
www.jenskelley.etsy.com
jenskelley@yahoo.com

42 // Jen Skelley is currently located in Boston. She trained at the Syracuse University College of Visual and Performing Arts in New York State and her clients have included Galison Mudpuppy, Graphique de France, American Girl, Mattel and John Lewis. Jen has also illustrated books and her work for Sweet'N Low's nationwide campaign was used across various media, including bus stops and magazines. She has also designed for the Christmas season at Waitrose. In the future she would like to continue working in the children's book industry and expand into more textile-based work.

Top / Sandi
Part of Jen's on-going Exotic Bird Series where delicate little birds each have different decorative flourishes within their oversized tales. Hand-drawn and Gocco printed by hand.

Bottom / Mugs
A limited edition screen-print from a hand-drawing created for a coffee themed art show in Philadelphia. Each cup is filled with visual interest and has a different shape.

Opposite / Garden
Jen's floral pattern is bright, cheerful and loosely drawn, demonstrating how effective outlines can be for defining motifs.

Jenean Morrison

www.jeneanmorrison.net
shop.jeneanmorrison.net
info@jeneanmorrison.com

43 // Jenean Morrison is from Duncan, Oklahoma, but is now located in Memphis, Tennessee after attending the University of Memphis. Jenean loves nature as well as cityscapes, and therefore loves to combine organic and structured elements with lots of detail and complex touches in her designs. She has a vivid memory and frequently draws on memories of the designs she saw as a child growing up in the 1970s. She also loves to look at fashion and home decor magazines for inspiration as well as design books with patterns compiled from different regions and eras. Jenean has licensed her work to companies such as FreeSpirit Fabric, Fisher-Price, Sigg, Momenta Scrapbooking, and The Rug Market. Apart from design she also likes to paint and has worked on collections belonging to the Mirage and Bellagio hotels in Las Vegas. She would like to move further into the home decor market and see her designs on bicycles – and maybe one day even on a Volkswagen Beetle!

Design Heroes:
Charles and Ray Eames, Verner Panton, Alexander Girard, George Nelson, Lucienne Day.

Above / Metropolis
Jenean has combined stylized floral and abstract elements and repeated them to form highly detailed, unconventional diagonal stripes.

Opposite / Starbright
Because of the complexity of this design, Jenean chose a limited colour palette featuring three shades of teal and white. It is inspired by tile designs from Portugal and Havana.

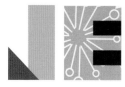

Jennifer Ellory

www.jennyellory.co.uk
www.jennyellory.blogspot.com
jennyellory@hotmail.com

44 // Jennifer Ellory grew up surrounded by vintage pattern and colour thanks to her antique-dealer father who taught her to appreciate them from an early age. She studied Surface Pattern Design at Staffordshire University and is now based in the beautiful city of Bath. Jennifer works for a variety of British and international retailers, designing stationery and gift wrap, greeting cards, tableware, children's fashion and craft projects for magazines. The blossom products and designs featured here were designed by Jennifer for Portico Designs, from concept through to print, as an exclusive stationery and gifting range for Waterstone's.

Top / Autumn Buds
Bright pinks and acid limes offer the strongest contrast with the dark autumnal background in this cheerful, striking floral pattern.

Bottom / Blossom Range
These products were designed by Jennifer for Portico Designs, for Waterstone's. The range included paper products such as notebooks, playing cards, a writing set, storage tins, umbrellas, pens and more.

Opposite / Blossom
A lively floral designed exclusively for Waterstone's. It was inspired by blooming bouquets, and was created using a contemporary, muted summer palette.

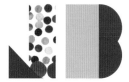

Jenny Bowers

www.jennybowers.co.uk
www.peepshow.org.uk

45 // Jenny Bowers has recently
moved back to Gloucestershire
after 12 years in London. Before
that she studied in Manchester
for a degree in Illustration and
Animation, and also at the Royal
College of Art in London for a
master's in Animation. Jenny joined
the Peepshow Collective in 2003
and since then has been working as a
freelance illustrator, art director and
prop-maker for film and television.
She also creates art prints for
exhibitions and galleries. Jenny is
inspired by her fellow illustrators at
Peepshow and has worked with
clients such as Kate Spade, Elle
Decoration, White Stuff, Penguin,
The RHS, Channel 4 and the BBC.
Jenny is represented in New York by
Art Department.

Design Heroes:
Paul Rand, Sister Corita, Alexander
Girard, Charles and Ray Eames.

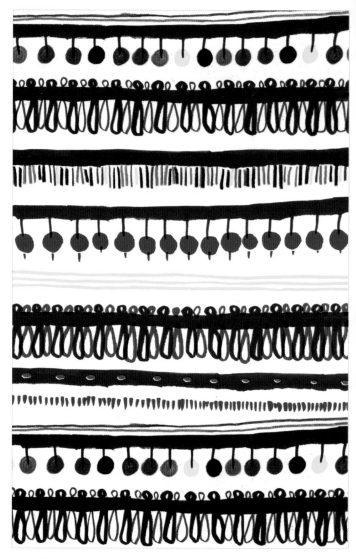

Above / Trim
Created as a textile design, Jenny has
made a stripe layout using colourful
illustrations of fabric trims.

Opposite top / Baubles
Created as a Christmas 2009 card for
the Peepshow Collective's online shop,
it features bold and loosely painted
bauble decorations.

Opposite bottom / Festive Fruit
Commissioned by Waitrose as part of its
Christmas 2009 packaging and
merchandise, Christmas greens and deep
reds create the perfect festive mood for
these hand-drawn fruit.

45 / Jenny Bowers

Above / Feet
Commissioned for a Howies clothing
catalogue, Jenny has filled the simple
shapes of the legs and feet with lively
and interesting patterns.

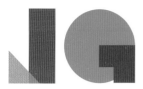

Jess Greenfield

www.peepingtompaper.com.au
www.etsy.com/shop/peepingtompaper
jess@peepingtompaper.com.au

46 // Jess Greenfield is located in Brisbane, Australia. She graduated in 2008 with a degree in Design from the Queensland College of Art and now runs a business called Peeping Tom Paper, which was born to satisfy and combine her love of all things pattern, paper and colour. Peeping Tom Paper has lots of stockists in Australia and an Etsy shop online. When talking of her work Jess says, 'I like to think my designs are slightly retro and, most important, very colourful!' She would love to dabble in textiles and see some of her designs on cloth.

Design Heroes:
Lucienne Day, Sanna Annukka, Paul Rand.

Top / We Are Family
Jess is inspired by geometric shapes and bold colour. She enjoys joining basic shapes together to create stylized designs and patterns.

Bottom / Flower Face
Created as a greeting card for Peeping Tom, this retro bloom is reminiscent of the 1960s.

Top / Tweet Heart
The very first design which started Peeping Tom Paper. Two colourful geometric birds sit back to back.

Bottom left / Upside Down Cat
Inspired by a cat Jess once looked after that spent more time hanging upside down from things then she did being upright.

Bottom right / Elanor
The most popular Peeping Tom design. Jess likes to use recognizable animals in her work and give them a quirky character of their own.

Jessica Jones

www.jessicajonesdesign.com
www.howaboutorange.blogspot
jessica@jessicajonesdesign.com

47 // Jessica Jones grew up in rural Minnesota and graduated with a Design Communication degree from the University of Minnesota. Now located in Evanston in the Chicago area, Jessica's main work is designing corporate identities and marketing collateral for businesses, but she enjoys creating patterns when she gets a little extra time. Jessica's fabrics have been used on a variety of retail products, from Reese Li handbags to chairs at The Land of Nod. She also designs jacquard ribbons for J. Caroline Designs, which are sold in many retail shops around the United States. Jessica loves Scandinavian and mid-century furniture, tablewares and graphic design and is also inspired by nature and city architecture. As part of her work is designing logos for clients, she suspects the constant practice of paring down an idea into a simple graphic mark influences how she designs her patterns as well. Her dream commission would be to design tableware.

Design Heroes:
Alexander Girard, Stig Lindberg, Lucienne Day.

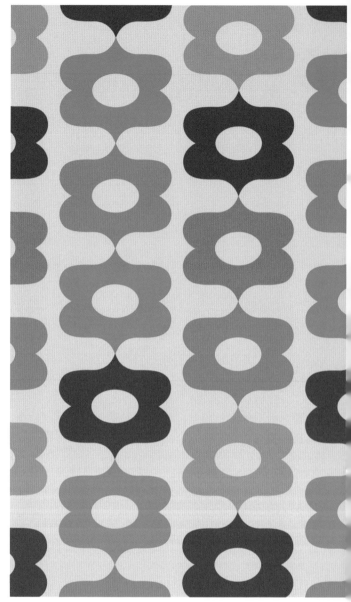

Above / Calliope
All of the designs shown here were created in Adobe Illustrator and printed on decorator-weight fabric. This design for Braemore was 'Inspired by horse-drawn gilded wagons that housed steam calliopes in circuses and parades.'

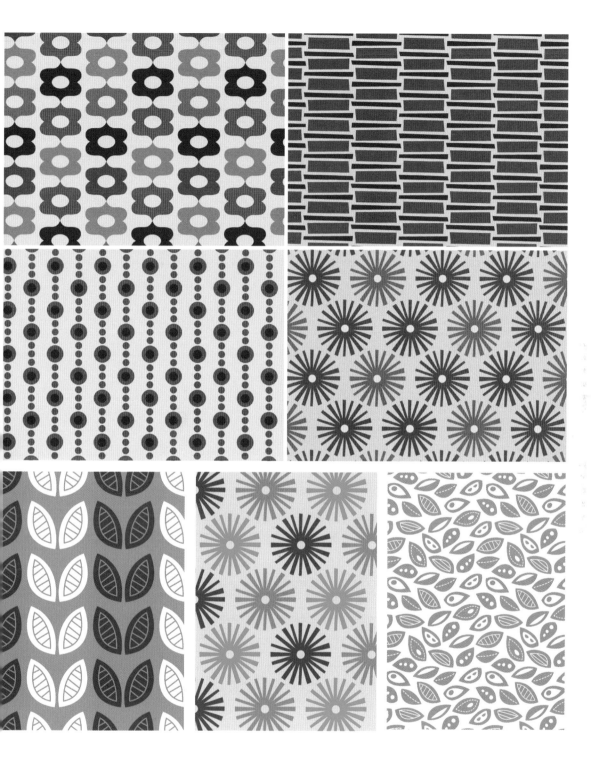

Top / Amusement Park Collection
Geometric, retro prints inspired by old-fashioned carnivals, for Braemore.

Bottom right / Leaflet
'Inspired by the first new leaves on sprouting seeds,' for J. Caroline Designs.

Bottom middle / Fireworks
'A happy burst of fireworks over an invisible seaside boardwalk,' for Braemore.

Bottom left / Herb
'A scattering of abstract leaves that could be mint and basil,' for J. Caroline Designs.

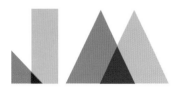

Jill McDonald

www.jillmcdonalddesign.com
www.jillmcdonald.blogspot.com
info@jillmcdonalddesign.com

48 // Jill Mcdonald Design is based in Kansas City, Missouri. After graduating from the Rhode Island School of Design with a degree in Textile Design, Jill went on to work in New York for BabyGap before returning to Kansas to work at Hallmark. Now running her own studio, Jill produces designs for children's books, stationery, bedding, scrapbooking and more. Clients have included The Land of Nod, Pottery Barn Kids and Target. She finds inspiration in colour, music and her family. Jill's ambition for the future is to paint cards, make her own ceramic pots and open a flower shop!

Design Heroes:
Mary Blair

Top / Beautiful Birds
Designed to capture the mood of early spring, this pattern was created in Photoshop by Jill McDonald and Elizabeth Sims for the Surtex show. The design was sold to Michaels Stores.

Opposite / Charming Floral
Although this is a floral print, it was created in January with a wintry theme using elements such as woven tweed effect to give it a sense of warmth and richness.

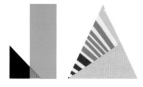

Jonathan Adler

www.jonathanadler.com

49 //   Jonathan Adler is originally from New Jersey where he became interested in pottery at a young age, begging his parents to buy him a wheel and kiln. In the 1990s he moved to New York and worked for a few years in the film industry before returning to his first love – making pots. Jonathan sold his first designs to Barneys in 1994 and opened his own store in Manhattan in 1998. It wasn't long before he had moved into designing his own furniture and accessories, and taking on interior design projects. More store openings followed and Jonathan now sells his products all over the world. He has also worked as a design judge on American television and published several books. He is fascinated by needlepoint design, chinoiseries, Scandinavian pottery, mid-century design, neoclassicism, bold colours and groovy graphics. All of these influences inform his work.

Design Heroes:
David Hicks, Bjorn Wiinblad, Alexander Girard.

Top / Square Pegs
This simple pattern is made fabulous by use of scale and colour.

Bottom / Bargello Diamond
Jonathan's passion for design means he is interested in referencing all eras and styles and, in doing so, creates classic patterns with his own twist.

Top / Bargello Hazard
Masterful use of geometrics makes this design a perfect example of symmetry and repetition. The motif is strikingly simple if seen in isolation but in repeat it becomes hypnotic.

Bottom / Bargello Hazard Hand-Drawn
Using the same motif as before but this time rotated, the shapes tessellate together like a jigsaw.

Opposite / Acapulco
Created for a range of stationery, this design possibly
has influences from South American folk art and is filled
with movement.

Above / Sun Motifs
Created as a fun print for children's wallpaper in the Jonathan
Adler Junior collection. The colours are appealing for either
boys or girls and the variety of sun motifs is quite absorbing.

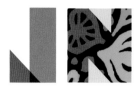

Julia Nielsen

www.pryldesign.se
julia@pryldesign.se

50 // Julia Nielsen is based in Stockholm but previously studied Visual Communication Design at Middlesex University in London. Julia is represented in the United Kingdom by The Bright Agency and her clients have included Boots, Designtorget, Carlton, American Greetings and Phaidon. She first worked as a graphic designer in London, then as a freelance illustrator in Germany, and now as a product designer in Sweden. Julia finds working across different disciplines keeps her inspired and she designs a variety of products for her own collaborative company Pryl, ('thingie' in Swedish). Pryl's style is bold colours, 1970s childhood nostalgia, beautiful patterns, vintage fabric reused in new contexts, quirky jewellery and design gifts.

Design Hero:
Lotta Kuhlhorn.

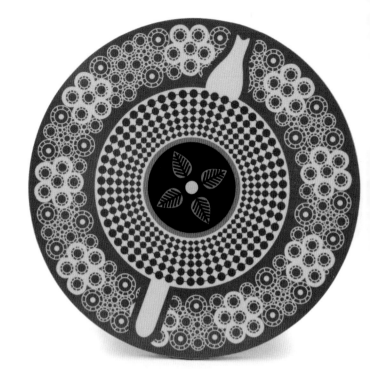

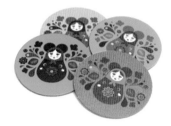

Top / Breakfast In Bed Pot stand designed for Designtorget, featuring a clever aerial view of a teapot with a modern geometric lacy style pattern.

Middle / Mouse Matryoshka These coasters and mouse mat are decorated with tiny colourful Russian dolls, who unusually have mouse ears, and are elaborated with Swedish-style Kurbits patterns, for Pryl Design.

Bottom / Owl Bag Green tote bag with a single colour motif which Julia describes as a 'slightly angry owl' for Pryl Design.

Top / Animal Cards
These cards were designed, produced and sold to shops through Julia's product design company Pryl Design. They have been offset printed and hand-assembled with an embroidered text tag.

Bottom / Clover Cutting-Board and Tea Towels
These large mod blooms have a retro Scandinavian feel and were produced in Sweden for Pryl Design.

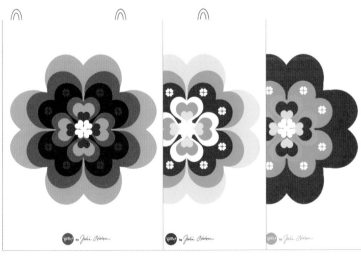

50 / Julia Nielsen

Opposite / Heart Scribble
Julia's hand-drawn scribble pattern takes on a softer, more feminine look in this colourway, printed on coasters for Pryl Design.

Above / Casino Scribble
A colourful pattern using rainbow brights contrasted with a black ground that was printed on postcards and coasters for Pryl Design.

Junzo Terada

www.comes-graphic.jp
www.beautifulday3000.com
comes@par.odn.ne.jp
takemura@beautifulday3000.com

51 // Junzo Terada is based in Osaka, Japan where he has worked as a graphic designer for many years before starting his own studio, Comes Graphic. Junzo designs and illustrates a wide range of products such as stationery, fabric, toys, book and album covers and tote bags – all of which can be found in the Comes Mart store he owns in Osaka. He has various clients in Japan and has also worked closely with Chronicle Books in the United States. Junzo is inspired by music, movies, books, fashion, and he loves well designed packaging and advertisements. Junzo is represented by the Tokyo based agency It's A Beautiful Day.

Design Hero:
Pushpin Studio.

Top /
Animal Adventures Cover
Junzo's design looks stunning on the cover of this sticky notes set published by Chronicle Books. All the motifs are arranged tightly packed in rows and, like all his designs shown here, it was hand-drawn and then scanned, coloured and processed in Photoshop.

Bottom / Magical Menagerie
Magical Menagerie is a wonderful box of 20 flat-packed card animals that form 3D sculptures simply by slotting together. Each animal is decorated in one of Junzo's fabulous geometric patterns.

Top left /
Happy Animal Time
The cover of this postcard set published by Chronicle Books features just one of Junzo's many cute animal characters which invoke a sense of magic and nostalgia.

Top right / Animal Greetings
Junzo's characters and patterns are given a chance to shine as individual pieces in this collection of Mix & Match stationery published by Chronicle Books.

Bottom /
Birds In Flight Mobile
Stylish patterns are put to good use on this bird mobile also from Chronicle Books. Different designs are used on the head, body, wings and tail to make it as visually stimulating for young eyes as possible.

Left / Elephant/Cat/Chicken
Three of the card animals
from Junzo's Magical
Menagerie.

Opposite / Animal Adventures
Inside the Sticky Notes
pack we can see the beautiful
stylized shapes of Junzo's
animals as they are isolated
and arranged on gridded
paper.

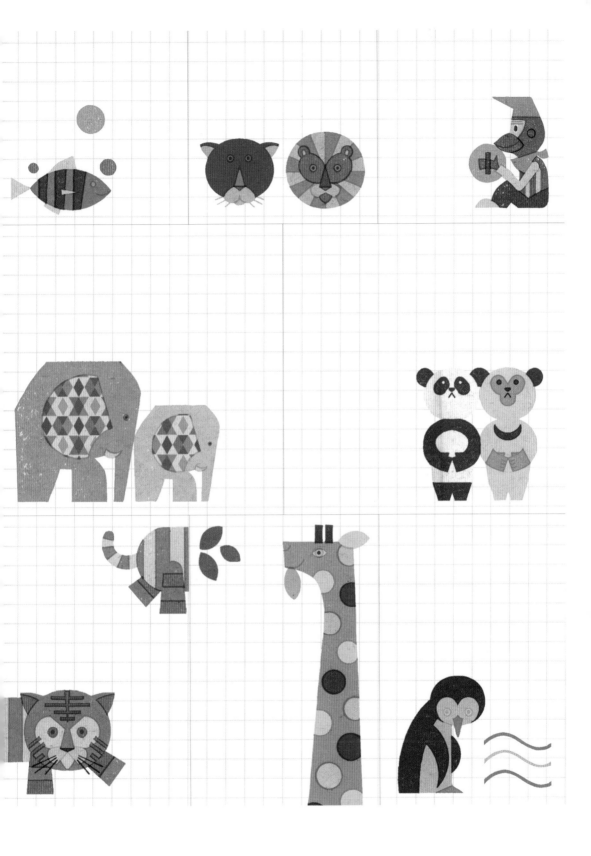

Jurianne Matter

www.juriannematter.nl
http://juriannematter.blogspot.com
info@juriannematter.nl

52 // Jurianne Matter is based in a village called Bussum, 20 minutes outside of Amsterdam. She studied Interior Styling at the Artemis Academy in Amsterdam and spent five years working for IKEA as a stylist. Jurianne now concentrates on designing paper products with beautiful pattern designs and runs her own wholesale company selling them. Everything is printed and produced in Holland and is eco-friendly. She begins the design process with a mood board and her work is informed by a love of Scandinavia, mid-century modern design, nature, and almost forgotten folkloric traditions and rituals. In the future she would like to branch out designing her own textile range – eco-cotton and fair trade of course!

Design Heroes:
Scholten en Baijings, Orla Kiely, Patricia Urquiola, Sanna Annukka, Roddy & Ginger, Sukie, Inaluxe.

Top / Blom Paper Flowers
The starting point for Blom was to create a design that would fit with a light, bright mid-century modern interior with lots of vintage Finnish ceramics.

Bottom / Blom Packs
The flowers have been made so that they can easily be pressed out of A5 card and threaded onto wire.

Above / Blom Cakes
Jurianne suggests attaching her flowers to a cocktail stick to
turn fairy cakes into trendy treats.

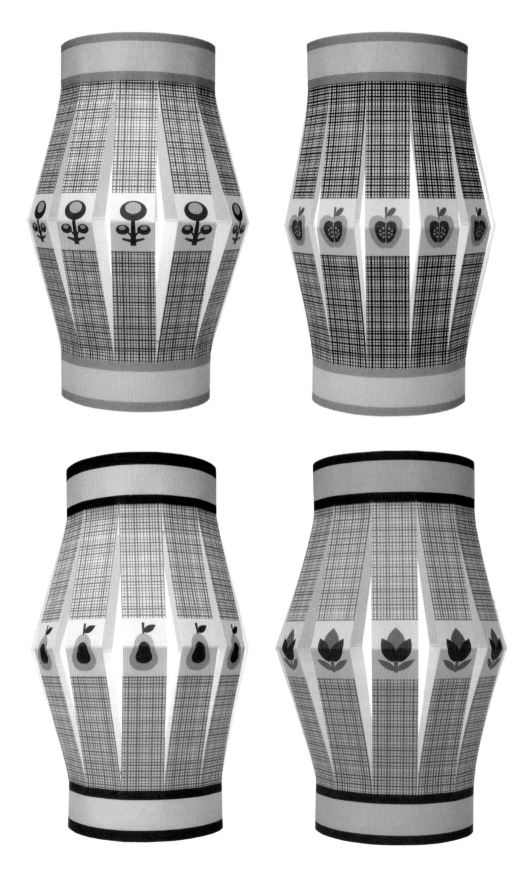

52 / Jurianne Matter

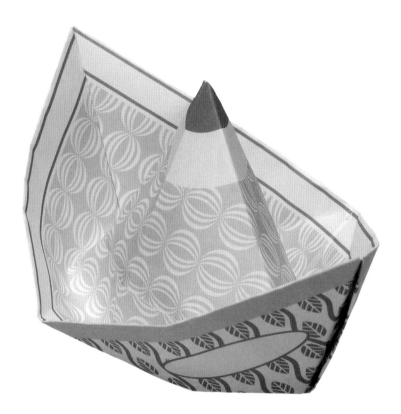

Opposite / Lanterns
When Jurianne visited Orla Kiely's store in Covent Garden she was in awe, and it proved to be very inspirational in the design of her Lanterns. They can be used flat for greeting cards and are easily folded to create the lantern around a tea-light glass. Photographs by Heidi de Wit.

Above / Little Wishboats
Designed to look like a nostalgic treasure or a souvenir of your childhood, these paper boats can be written on before folding with a personal message. For each product, Jurianne will create hundreds of pattern swatches and use only her favourite on the final pieces. Photographs by Heidi de Wit.

K&Company

www. kandcompany.com

53 // Kay Stanley and Curt Seymour founded K&Company in 1996 with the development of a unique personalized system called Frame-a-Name®. Today K&Company is well known for its fabulous scrapbooking products. They manufacture albums, scrapbook papers, stickers and a huge variety of embellishments. K&Company products are available in over 23 countries and in nearly 5,000 independent gift, scrapbook, craft and retail stores in the United States. All the designs featured here are from their Poppy Seed collection and demonstrate how each pattern in a series is interesting enough to stand on its own and yet co-ordinate perfectly.

Top / Poppy Seed
Rub Ons With Gems
Floral elements found within the paper pattern designs are used in these rub-ons and topped off with gems.

Bottom / Poppy Seed
To make a contrast from the light pastels this print has a lovely dark background colour. The flowers are sketchy for a hand drawn look and very deliberately off register from the solid colour below.

Opposite / Dream Catcher
A light and airy delicate medallion style design in pastel mint green. Produced as part of K&Company's designer paper pad.

Opposite / Poppy Seed Designer Paper Pad
This striking floral was chosen for the front cover of Poppy
Seed Designer Pad as it is eye-catchingly bold. Although the
style of flower is different, there are still the unifying elements
of the colour palette and outline effect.

Above / Floral Line Art
The whole of this pattern is drawn in outline and several of the
Dream Catcher motifs also appear in this floral design to create
a unifying factor for the two prints.

Kate Clarke

kateclarkelondon.com
info@kateclarkelondon.com

54 // A Londoner by birth, Kate Clarke is currently based in East Dulwich where she shares an artists' studio and generally makes a lot of mess creating her screen-printed products. Kate studied Visual Communication at Leeds College of Art and Design and graduated in 2000. She has been a children's book cover designer for ten years, working for Random House, Penguin and Bloomsbury. At university Kate discovered screen-printing, fell instantly in love and has been doing it during evenings and at weekends ever since. She starts the design process by cutting out coloured paper shapes and laying them out all over the living room floor. Kate is inspired by 1950s design, in particular Scandinavian and Japanese design, and is also fond of 1950s and 60s book covers and anything handmade. 'I love the medium of screen-printing' she says, 'the possibilities are endless.' In the future, Kate would like to design her own range of bedding and wallpaper.

Design Heroes:
Dick Bruna, Lucienne Day,
Olle Eksell.

Opposite top / Stalk Print
This print was designed
with a cushion cover in mind.
It had to be big and bold,
using fresh green combined
with soft pink. The edges
have the distinctive look of
cut paper for added interest.
Papercut screen-print.

Opposite bottom /
Retro Kitchen
Kate wanted this design to
reflect her love of 1950s fabric
but to be modern and fresh
and to bring a flash of colour
into the kitchen. Papercut
screen-print.

Left /
Poppy Print in Yellow & Red
A papercut screen-print
created as a cushion design.
Kate wanted the design to be
simple and graphic, retro but
with a contemporary twist.

Kate Larsen

www.boxofbirds.co.uk
kate@boxofbirds.co.uk

55 // Kate Larsen is based in Kent, just outside London. She studied at the Ravensbourne College of Design and Communication taking a degree in Visual Information Design. One side of Kate's family is Danish, so there has always been a strong Scandinavian influence in her life and there are quite a few designers and creative people in her family, further fuelling her interest in design and illustration. For inspiration, Kate reads interior and design magazines and blogs, and she is also influenced by fashion, packaging and photography. Clients have included Topshop, Mothercare, The Body Shop and Cardmix. Freelance graphic design work is organized through Kate directly and for illustration work she is represented by Eye Candy.

Above / Hatched Flowers
Kate always hand draws elements of a pattern first, then scans them in ready to re-draw with Illustrator and to produce the final design.

Opposite / Flower Buds
A vintage-feel print inspired by mid-century design, this stylized floral is from Kate's own personal work.

Katie Bailey

www.smile-recipe.net
http://smilerecipe.etsy.com
katie@smile-recipe.net

56 //   Katie Bailey is based in Ontario, Canada where she works on her design brand Smile Recipe. Katie studied Graphic Design at Algonquin College in Ottawa and is influenced by *kawaii* style, fairy tales, and folk art. Through her Etsy shop Katie designs, makes and sells a variety of items from pin badges to pencil cases. In the future she would like to create a fabric line of her own.

Above / Petite Wild Flowers
A formal repeat of geometric flowers pick up on Katie's love of retro design.

Opposite top left / Favourite Things
All of Katie's patterns were created entirely in Illustrator with the aid of her 'trusty drawing tablet'. Usually they are unique one-offs, but with these Katie set out to create multiple patterns that were all very different but still complementary.

Opposite top right / Nearing The Village
The folk theme is evident in this design which features village houses and windmills – both classic motifs in Eastern European and Dutch tradition – but given a totally modern twist.

Opposite bottom left / Well Kept Gardens
Since Katie likes to sew and make products from her artwork, she always takes into account how the design will look printed as fabric. This is a perfect example of a repeat with geometric flowers sitting in honeycomb vignettes.

Opposite bottom right / Flowercomb
The first design in this series has a retro, folksy look with a touch of *kawaii* which is Katie's favourite artistic style.

Kelly Hyatt
and Lagom

www.lagomdesign.co.uk
www.hyattassociates.co.uk
hello@lagomdesign.co.uk

57 //   Kelly Hyatt is the designer behind Lagom, a publisher of contemporary greeting cards. Kelly designs many of Lagom's ranges himself but also scours the world to publish the work of other great designers. Kelly studied Graphic Design and Print at De Montfort and Loughborough Universities and then Fine Art at Nottingham. As well as working for Lagom he also works on a broad range of freelance projects, from rebranding, illustration, advertising and websites to interior design. Clients vary from large corporate companies to individuals. Scandinavian design is Kelly's biggest influence but he also loves music and architecture, fashion and food. Kelly is currently based in Paris.

Design Heroes:
Achille Castiglioni, Junzo Terada, Hans Wegner, Alexander Girard, Arne Jacobsen, Charles and Ray Eames.

Above / Kyoto
From the Boda greeting card collection this flower has great depth thanks to clever use of layering. Printed using special colours and metallic inks on recycled board.

Opposite top left / Orka
A graphic floral stem print design produced in Illustrator and Photoshop. From the Hygge (pronounced 'hoo-ga') range.

Opposite top right / Lærke
Graceful birds embellished with flourishes and curlicues on a greetings card from the Hygge collection. Like all Lagom cards it is printed with vegetable based inks.

Opposite bottom left / Blue cake
Geometric shapes are expertly placed to create a stylized cake design produced in Illustrator and Photoshop.

Opposite bottom right / Aina
From the Hygge range of greeting cards this design uses just two colours to create a pattern of graphic medallions. Printed with special inks and spot varnish on recycled board using environmental print technology.

Overleaf left / One Dove
A Scandinavian inspired design from the Boda range of everyday greeting cards.

Overleaf right / Vår kärlek
A Scandinavian-style design that uses clean lines and flat shapes to build up a stylish look. Produced as a greeting card for the Boda collection.

Opposite / Opoponax
A beautifully detailed pattern created for gift wrap by Stockholm-based designer Hanna Werning. It has clear folkloric influences within the two repeated vignettes.

Top / Yellow Summer
Flat colour and stylized flower shapes give this design a modern look. Arranged in formal rows like an abacus and interspersed with dots, it was created for gift wrap.

Bottom left / Squirrel Love
From the fun Zootown range of greeting cards. The tree design is not intended to be realistic but expressive and dynamic.

Bottom right / Zootown Owl
A bold graphic owl detailed with triangle feathers and a colour palette to contrast with the moonlit sky.

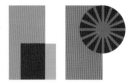

Lab Partners

www.lp–sf.com
sarah@lp-sf.com

58 //   Lab Partners are Ryan
Meis and Sarah Labieniec who
both studied Graphic Design and
Illustration at the Ringling College
of Art and Design in Sarasota.
Together they work on design
and illustration projects from their
base in the San Francisco Bay area.
Clients have included Penguin
Books, The New York Times,
Clementine Paper, and Hewlett
Packard. Their inspiration often
comes from mid-century animation,
travelling, textiles, cooking, people
watching and their two cats. Their
dream job would be to design a big
campaign to bring back the glory
and excitement of train travel in
the United States.

Design Heroes:
Yurio Seki, Herbert Leupin,
Alice and Martin Provensen.

Above / Pen Pals
'Nothing compares to getting
a good old-fashioned letter in
the mail,' say Ryan and Sarah,
and this was the inspiration
for this letterpress print
created in three colours. Part
of a series this particular one
features a llama.

Opposite / Rain Tree
Simple curves, circles and
shapes give a geometric feel
to the fruit and flowers in this
bold silkscreen poster which
was designed as a celebration
of spring and new growth.

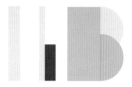

Lara Brehm

www.larabrehm.com
www.larabrehm.blogspot.com
larabrehm@gmail.com

59 // Illustrator and graphic designer Lara Brehm is originally from Hamburg in Germany but went on to study design in both Spain and France. Lara now lives and works in Paris where she is represented by top Paris-based studio Atelier LZC and, amongst others, by New York's Juna Studio.

Top / Like a Fish in the Sea
Fun looking fish are cleverly given a structure by using seaweed.

Bottom /
Vintage Flower in Ochre
A simple stylized floral is filled with texture and the colour is pure retro.

Opposite / A Touch of Spring
Silhouettes of plants and flowers create a simple pattern whose beauty is brought out in the colour choices.

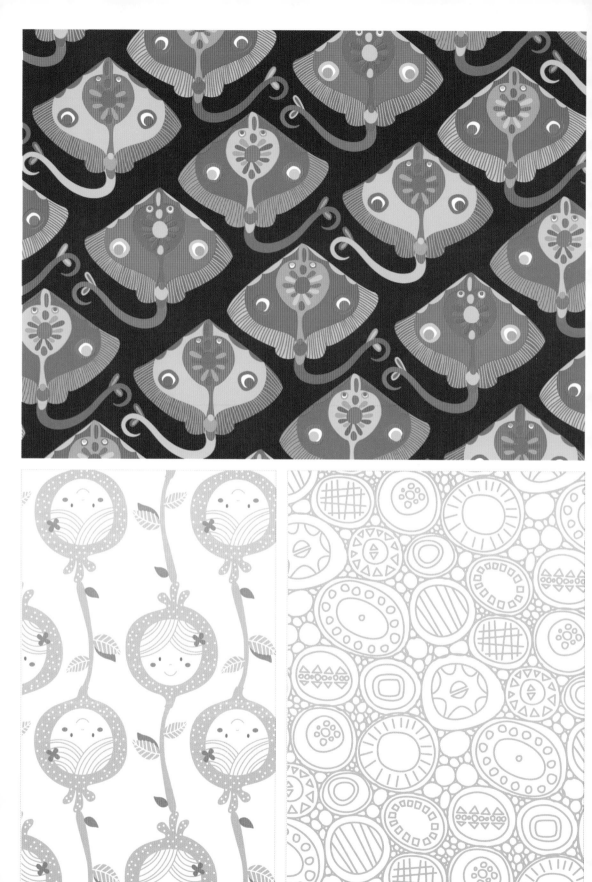

Opposite top / Neon Rayfish
Lara uses the distinctive shape of the ray fish to tessellate this boldly coloured design.

Opposite bottom left /
Flower Kid
Lara has created a whimsical style for this design that features a cute face in a flower linked together in a clever repeat.

Opposite bottom right /
Spinning Bubbles
No space is left unfilled in this detailed pattern featuring creative interpretations of bubbles.

Above / Feathers
A lovely sketchy-style abstract pattern using overlapping feathers.

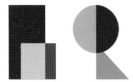

Lemon Ribbon

www.lemonribbon.com
info@lemonribbon.com

60 // Lemon Ribbon is a creative youth-focused design studio based on the outskirts of London owned by Melanie Bullock and Edward Weale. Melanie studied at the University of East London where her final collection involved bright digitally-printed sportswear. After a successful career working for various British retail clients and suppliers in childrenswear, Melanie set up Lemon Ribbon with Edward in 2009. The studio was an enormous success and has grown steadily since. Lemon Ribbon creates distinctive designs for a wide range of children's products including wall coverings, nursery products, greeting cards and stationery. They also represent a team of talented British designers under the Lemon Ribbon umbrella selling seasonal collections to fashion, apparel, home decor and stationery markets. Clients range from worldwide retailers and manufacturers to small independent brands and products.

Design Heroes:
Ed Emberley, Charley Harper, Kandinsky, William Morris.

Above / Butterfly Farm Wall
Inspired by lickable wallpaper! This contemporary wall covering was created in Illustrator for the nursery wall, following one of the main looks of the Lemon Ribbon brand of creating patterns in rows.

Bottom / Animal Sanctuary
Created in Illustrator this super cute design uses word pattern fills, opacity mixes, muted shades and Lemon Ribbon's characters to build an environment for any child to lose themselves in.

Top left / Leo the Lion
Lovely Leo is one of the first
original characters created
under the umbrella of Lemon
Ribbon. He started the whole
family of animals, created by
layering opacities of colour in
Illustrator and using pattern
fills for the background and
mane.

Top middle / Floral Telephone
Designed for the Lemon
Ribbon website using pattern
fills, it creates a fun and
friendly image.

Top right / Floral Symmetry
A lovely modern folk floral
pattern created in Illustrator
from the Lemon Ribbon
brand collection.

Bottom / Floral and
Birdie Sampler
Inspired by cross-stitch
sampler patterns from old
cushions and wall hangings,
this design is from the Lemon
Ribbon brand collection.

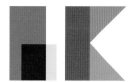

Linda Ketelhut

www.lindaketelhut.com
www.lindaketelhut.etsy.com
www.lillarogers.com

61 // Linda Ketelhut is originally from Detroit but now lives in Austin, Texas. Linda is a self-taught illustrator who works with gouache, wood, fabric as well as working digitally, often combining techniques. She is inspired by the use of space in design – how it's used, the moods it creates and the placement of things within it, such as the colour and texture. Linda also finds inspiration in nature, travelling, details, music and people. She is represented by Lilla Rogers and clients have included Chronicle Books, Random House, Graphique de France, and Magic Murals. The designs featured here are all from her personal work. Her dream commission would be to collaborate with a fashion designer on a clothing line but she is also interested in designing rugs and fabrics for the home.

Design Heroes:
Paola Ivana Suhonen of IVANAhelsinki, Orla Kiely, Maija Louekari, Lucienne Day.

Top / Bloom
Linda captures a vintage feel through the use of a bold colourful graphic combined with rough, worn wood textures in this digital print inspired by screen-printing.

Bottom / Tangerine
Personal work, wood and linen with digital illustration.

Top left / Lily
One in a collection of
nature-inspired mod flower
illustrations. Elements were
hand-drawn and painted
with gouache then scanned
into the computer to create
a digital collage incorporating
wood and linen.

Top right / Tulip
A collage from her mod
flower collection. The dark
wood background throws the
bold semi-circle elements
forward as she perfectly mixes
soft hand-painted lines with
accurate digital ones.

Bottom / Peony
A design from Linda's nature-
inspired flower illustrations.
Combining gouache, wood,
linen and digital illustration.

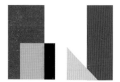

Lisa Jones Studio

www.lisajonesstudio.com
www.lisajonesstudio.bigcartel.com
info@lisajonesstudio.com

62 // Lisa Jones is based in what she calls 'the creative hub' of Hackney, East London where she works with her partner Edward Underwood. Lisa attended both Middlesex University and Central St Martins and now runs the Lisa Jones Studio producing a range of greeting cards, silkscreen prints, tea towels and mugs. For inspiration Lisa says nothing quite gets her in the zone like flicking through Conran's series of interior lookbooks from the 1970s. Client based projects have included a limited edition art print for the Victoria and Albert Museum and two children's books with ethical publishers, Silver Jungle. Her dream commission would be to design a collection of postage stamps.

Design Heroes:
Olle Eksell, Tom Eckersley.

Top / Nightowls
Silkscreen print. Another paper collage, whose elements are scanned into Photoshop. Lisa has a penchant for old posters so it made perfect sense to utilize that winning layout, albeit without text and with nothing to promote.

Bottom / Raccoon
Silkscreen greetings card. Lisa says, 'although it's the stripped-back efficiency of handmade cards that some people respond to, it's also a look born of necessity; with each silkscreened colour representing extra labour, it's prudent to limit the palette.' A combination of paper collage and pastel crayon scanned into Photoshop and output as transparencies for silkscreening by hand.

Top left / Pablo
Lisa says of this Peacock design, that it 'makes no effort to conceal the influence of Scandinavian folk art, contemporary ceramics and the friendly, decorative illustration of yesteryear.' Lithographic greeting card printed with soy-based inks on recycled card.

Top right / Olaf
The stark monochrome of this range was intended to rein in the overall complexity of the designs and lend them a grown-up edge. A paper collage was vectored in Illustrator for a spot-colour litho on recycled stock with soy-based inks.

Bottom left / Town
Silkscreen print. Part of a larger design for gift wrap. Unmistakably English and probably coastal, it taps into a current trend for domestic modernism. A pencil drawing and paper collage scanned into Photoshop.

Bottom right / Leroy
One of six Kapok Creatures inspired by the soft toys fashioned by crafters throughout the 1960s and '70s. Regularly using garish or mismatched textile remnants and stuffed with kapok (a naturally occurring, cotton-like wadding), they still retain a certain homespun charm. The design is created by assembling scanned elements of wool, fabric and paper-collage in Photoshop. Lithographic greeting card printed with soy-based inks on recycled card.

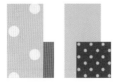

Liza Lewis

www.lizalew.co.uk
mail@lizalew.co.uk

63 // Liza Lewis is originally from Belgium but has been living in the United Kingdom for 18 years. She graduated with a diploma in Graphic Design from the Bournemouth Arts Institute in 2006. Now based in Southampton she is currently working as a freelance illustrator and graphic designer and has worked on a number of commissions for the gift and greeting card industry. Liza has also started creating various children's products and designing patterns for gift wrap and home furnishings. Inspiration comes from many sources including her children, dog, books, toys, music, art, fabrics and plants. She has a particular interest in children's illustration and enjoys creating new and exciting characters.

Top / Lots of Sausage Dogs
Liza has experimented with different pattern fills and colours in this quirky and colourful design with playful sausage dogs and little birds.

Bottom /
Flowers & Dragonflies
A colourful floral pattern design broken up by dancing dragonflies and using retro colours reminiscent of 1960s mod florals.

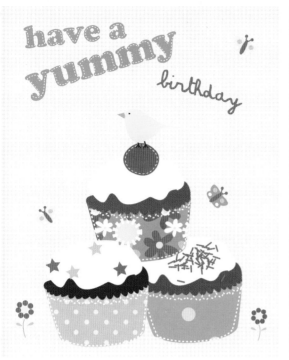

Top left / Yummy Cakes
Published by Soul from the Sherbet range. Cupcakes have been a phenomenal success on cards, fabrics, gifts and paper goods and Liza's are a beautiful example. The patterned paper cases, birds and butterflies add to the whimsical look.

Top right / With Love Heart
This card is part of a range of 28 Sherbet greeting cards published by Soul. The heart appears to be made of colourful fabrics and stitched to the card in this clever illustration.

Bottom left / Birthday Presents
Liza wanted a look that was slightly retro and cute, featuring a mix of patterns, and finished with sewing effect detail. For the Sherbet range.

Bottom right / Get Well Soon
A homespun gingham background with lots of apples – the traditional symbol for a get well card. For the Sherbet range.

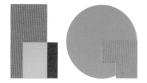

Lotta Glave

www.bengt-lotta.se
lotta@bengt-lotta.se

64 // Lotta Glave and her company Bengt & Lotta are based in Stockholm where they have a shop and studio. Lotta trained at the University College of Arts, Crafts and Design in Stockholm (Konstfack) and was a guest student at Chisholm Institute of Technology in Melbourne. For Bengt & Lotta she designs trays, candleholders, cards, jewellery and more. She also designs textile patterns and wool blankets for various clients including Klippan Yllefabrik, as well as paper products for Bookbinders Design. Lotta finds herself inspired by the everyday life around her, by her children, and also by traditional folk art. Her patterns are all hand-drawn and then scanned to suit production.

Top / Flower Power
Lollypop shaped flowers arranged in a drop repeat look bright and cheery on this fabric for Klippan Yllefabrik, and on trays and cards for Bengt & Lotta.

Bottom / Birds Red
A beautifully illustrated bird pattern whose shapes undulate and bend to fit together and create an all-over packed design. Used for fabric, paper napkins, trays, cutting boards and cards.

Opposite / Candy
A classic Lotta print of stylized sweets which have been pared down in true Scandinavian style. Used on trays, cutting boards and cards for Bengt & Lotta, a version with fewer colours was created for textiles at Klippan Yllefabrik.

Above / Alma
A whimsical floral pattern
with folk influences created as
a fabric for Klippan Yllefabrik.
This pattern was also used
on napkins, trays, cards and
dishcloths.

Right / Flower
A striking one colour floral
design on a dishcloth for
Office OCT in Japan.

Opposite / Orient
An abstract pattern fabric for
Klippan Yllefabrik and for
cards and trays for Bengt &
Lotta.

Louise Cunningham

www.louisecunningham.co.uk
www.louisecunninghamillustrator.
blogspot.com
louise@louisecunningham.co.uk

65 //   Louise Cunningham is
originally from Fife in Scotland
and graduated with a degree in
Visual Communication and an
Illustration diploma from the
Edinburgh College of Art.
Now based in Bristol she works
as a freelance illustrator and was
featured in *Images 34* (2010), the
design annual produced by the
Association of Illustrators. Besides
editorial work, Louise also produces
surface patterns, greeting cards,
and hand-lettering designs. Clients
have included John Lewis, Museums
& Galleries, *Ottobre* magazine,
Paperchase, Quire and Tigerprint.
One of her ambitions is to write
and illustrate a children's book.

Design Heroes:
Alice and Martin Provensen,
Eric Carle, Ezra Jack Keats,
Mark Hearld, Joan Eardley,
Brian Wildsmith.

Top / Doves
Saturated translucent colours contrast
perfectly with the cool grey background
on this greeting card for The Almanac
Gallery.

Bottom / Ducks
The transparent look of Louise's ducks
results in a wonderful overlapping effect
that has great appeal. Created in
Photoshop as a greeting card for Minty
Designs.

Top / Teacups
A simple design of a cup and saucer is brought to life with Louise's colour choices and layering effect. Produced as a fabric by Robert Kaufman.

Bottom / Cutlery
Designed as a bright and cheery fabric that is perfect for kitchen and quilt projects, part of a collection for Robert Kaufman.

Marimekko

www.marimekko.com
info@marimekko.fi

66 // Marimekko was founded by Armi and Viljo Ratia in Finland in 1951. By the late 1950s their fabrics were being exported to the United States with great success and were even worn by Jacqueline Kennedy during the 1960 presidential campaign. Soon their bold graphic patterns became recognizable around the world. They were renowned for their ultra-large 'supergraphic' patterns, in bright flat colours that often clashed, the most famous probably being Unikko by Maija Isola. Today the company designs, manufactures and markets high-quality clothing, interior decoration, textiles, bags, kitchenware and other accessories under the Marimekko brand, both in Finland and abroad.

Above / Tuliainan ('Souvenir')
Fabric print by Pia Holm for Marimekko, 2010. A lovely stylized floral design sketched by hand so that it has a loose informal feel.

Opposite /
Kanteleen Kutsu ('Call of Kantele')
Fabric print by Sanna Annukka for Marimekko, 2008. This bold graphic print tells stories from the Finnish national epic, The Kalevala. A Kantele is a plucked string instrument which the animals have gathered to listen to.

Opposite / Kippis ('Cheers')
Fabric print by Maija Louekari for Marimekko, 2008.
This pattern made of crystal glasses was originally intended
to decorate a porcelain mug. It uses flashes of colour overlaid
with black detailing.

Above / Siirtolapuutarha ('Allotment')
Fabric print by Maija Louekari for Marimekko, 2009.
Coloured flowers are overlaid with black outline and pattern.

Marina Molares

www.marinamolares.com
www.marinamolares.blogspot.com
marinamolares@gmail.com

67 // Marina Molares has a Spanish father, an American mother, and she has studied in England so she has quite a mix of cultural influences. She studied for a master's degree at the University of Leeds and also has a degree in Fine Art from the Universidad Complutense de Madrid, where she is now based. Marina's designs have been published in *Texitura*, one of the most important international pattern design magazines in the world. To be published in the magazine's trend forecast the designs had to meet a specific colour palette, which included a golden ink. Other clients have included Spanish label Hoss Intropia.

Design Hero:
Omo Tribe in Ethiopia.

Above / Love Doves
Created to fit the *Texitura* brief 'The Magical Beauty of Everyday Things'. Requirements included drawing animals with colourful lines for a fun trend, while leaving space for the imagination.

Opposite / Sunflower Seeds
Created for the brief on 'The Magical Beauty of Everyday Things' that had to do with looking at ordinary things with new eyes, as an alien might do.

Overleaf left / Long Haired Forest
From the *Texitura* trend 'Urban Field' where Marina was asked to think about vegetation and to use black ink for details.

Overleaf right / Metal Trees
Another design for *Texitura*'s 'Urban Field' where the brief was to interpret vegetation with an industrial look.

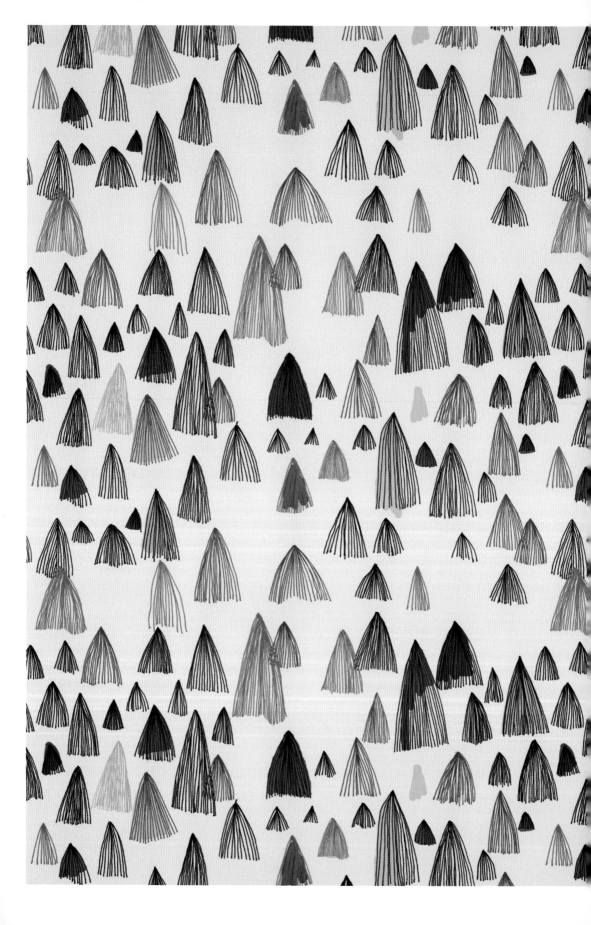

Mercedes Cortes

www.garabateoprints.blogspot.com
merche@gmail.com

68 // Mercedes Cortes is a
Spanish designer and illustrator
based in Barcelona. She works under
the studio name Garabateo Prints
and enjoys creating patterns for
clothing, tableware and accessories.
Mercedes is especially interested in
floral designs.

Above / Leaf Stripe
Rows of stem leaves are packed
with detail in a linear design
that uses coloured and white
backgrounds together.

Below / Geo Flowers
Great use of geometric forms
and dot inlays gives this design
a retro flavour.

Opposite top / Tulips
Another stem-based
arrangement – which always
gives a design great structure
– but this time the movement
and interest come from the
dot details on each flower.

Opposite bottom / Stems
Floral seed heads are
stylized against ellipses
with organically shaped
leaves for contrast.

Opposite / Rosettes
Dark and moody flowers with sharply angled leaves give this
print a cool edge.

Above / Tonal Flowers
Petals are divided up into different shades of blue and defined
by an outline to give light and dark to the print.

Mini Labo

www.minilabo.fr
contact@minilabo.fr

69 // Mini Labo are designers Caroline Diaz and Céline Héno who together with businesswoman Sophie Adary are a company based in Paris. Caroline and Céline were both students at the Duperré School of Art in Paris and have worked with clients such as Luminarc, La Redoute, Vertbaudet, Mon Petit Art, and their main licensee Atomic Soda. They are also working for Belle Maison, a mail order company in Japan which even held an exhibition of their designs at Printemps in Ginza, Tokyo. Mini Labo products include delightfully quirky soft toy characters, stationery, wall stickers and ceramics. Going forward the girls are giving up on production to concentrate purely on design. They would like to design a T-shirt collection for both women and children, as well as bedlinen, wallpaper and jewellery.

Design Heroes:
Nathalie Lété, Marc Boutavant, Jean-Michel Alberola, Dubuffet, Rob Ryan.

Top / Cache Cache ('Hide & Seek')
This pattern was designed for a small notebook, part of the Mini Labo collection for Atomic Soda.

Bottom left /
Fleur Des Champs ('Meadow Flowers')
Featuring a bird, flowers and poetry, this represents the Mini Labo universe all on one metal button.

Bottom right / Nous Deux ('The Two Of Us')
This rock'n'roll couple are a tribute to the French band Les Rita Mitsouko.

Top left /
Claire De Lune ('Moonlight')
Mini Labo sweetly illustrated
a little couple under a Parisian
moonlight, for a notebook
that forms part of their
collection for Atomic Soda.

Top right / Forest
A fabulous pattern inspired by
the forests of northern Europe
it has been used in several
products in the Mini Labo
collection for Atomic Soda.

Bottom left /
Les Amis ('Friends')
This Atomic soda notebook
gathers a lot of Mini Labo
characters – funny humanized
animals or creatures which
are always smiling.

Bottom right /
Lapin D'Avril ('April Rabbit')
A soft toy in felt and Liberty
fabrics from Mini Labo's
very first collection in 2004.
Designed as a tribute to Alice
in Wonderland's March hare.

Natalie Marshall

www.littleredowl.com.au
www.littleredowl.etsy.com
littleredowl@gmail.com

70 // Natalie Marshall lives in St.Kilda in Melbourne but has previously worked in design studios in London and New York. Natalie took a degree in Graphic Design at Monash University, with a major in Illustration. Her focus for many years was in corporate design for the financial sector with projects including annual reports and identity design, although Natalie always had a secret yearning to illustrate. Drawing has always been a love of hers and although she put it to one side for a few years, having children has inspired her to draw and create. She now runs Little Red Owl, freelancing for clients locally and internationally. Recent achievements include illustrating four children's books, creating her own range of 12 illustrated greeting cards and – a dream come true for her – designing fabric.

Design Hero:
Eric Carle.

Above / Jungle Counting Lion/
Jungle Counting Elephant
Like all of Natalie's designs featured here, these were created digitally in Adobe Illustrator. The retro feel animals are part of her fun series of three Jungle Counting illustrations for young boys.

Top left /
Birthday Animal Stack
Created for her range of Little
Red Owl greeting cards. The
animal stack is always popular
with children and Natalie
wanted it to exude fun and
happiness.

Top right / New Baby Owls
From her range of Little Red
Owl greeting cards. This
illustration using cheerful
owls to represent a family
was created specifically to be
suitable for either a new baby
boy or girl.

Bottom / Blue Pattern Owl
A beautifully stylized graphic
owl is framed by a border of
leaves in this vignette design
created as a personal piece.

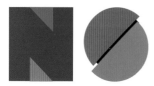

Niamh Smith

www.littleredtreacle.com
www.littleredtreacle.blogspot.com
littleredtreacle@hotmail.com

71 //   Niamh Smith is currently based in London where she works in Design at Topshop. In the evenings and at weekends she works on commissions and likes to keep her own work ticking along with new ideas. Originally from County Cavan in Ireland, Niamh studied Printed Textile Design at the National College of Art and Design, Dublin. After graduating she worked for CircleLine Design in London for five years, and then at Paul Smith for two years. Niamh's designs have been sold to fashion companies all over the world and have been seen at many catwalk shows.

Design Heroes:
Rob Ryan, Josef Frank,
Charley Harper.

Top & bottom / B, E, F, G
Niamh likes to create letters by designing beautiful imagery around the silhouette. She created all of these images in Adobe Photoshop using a drawing tablet to get greater control and more detail for an etched effect.

Opposite / Live Love Laugh!!
Niamh loves typography and pattern and by developing her unique style manages to successfully incorporate both into her stylish designs.

Overleaf / Home
Here Niamh uses a variety of patterns around the letters H, O,
M, E whether it be geometric, floral or even a scene.

Nicola Pearson

www.nicolapearson.blogspot.com
www.paperandcloth.net
nicolapearsondesign@yahoo.co.uk

72 // Nicola Pearson took a Foundation Arts course in Manchester to discover what area she wanted to pursue – only to discover that it actually made her want to pursue everything! So she opted for a really creative and open Decorative and Fine Arts Degree course at De Montfort University, Leicester. This enabled Nicola to work with multimedia fabrics, illustration, sculpture and wearable art. After graduating she moved into print and digital media and currently works producing designs for the Paper and Cloth studio. Clients have included Mamas & Papas, Adams, Peacocks, and Sainsbury's. Nicola feels that first and foremost she is inspired by the people with whom she works: 'I love brainstorming with other designers, sharing images and regaling stories.' She is also influenced by all sorts of illustration, pictures and stories from children's books, and fashion trends.

Design Heroes:
Vivienne Westwood, Barbara Hepworth, Andy Goldsworthy, Samantha Brian, Sue Murray (her first boss).

Above / Bird Floral
Created for her studio portfolio (and purchased by H&M Kids) for childrenswear. Nicola wanted a bright yet soft and cute look, with interesting small details that became apparent when examined more closely.

Opposite / Dot Spot Flowers
This print was developed by considering the use of colour first and foremost, and creating a pattern of bold yet pretty shapes to balance it. This palette is typical of Nicola's work – muted soft backgrounds of grey, or neutrals, or faded out pastel colours with tutti frutti style brights popped in.

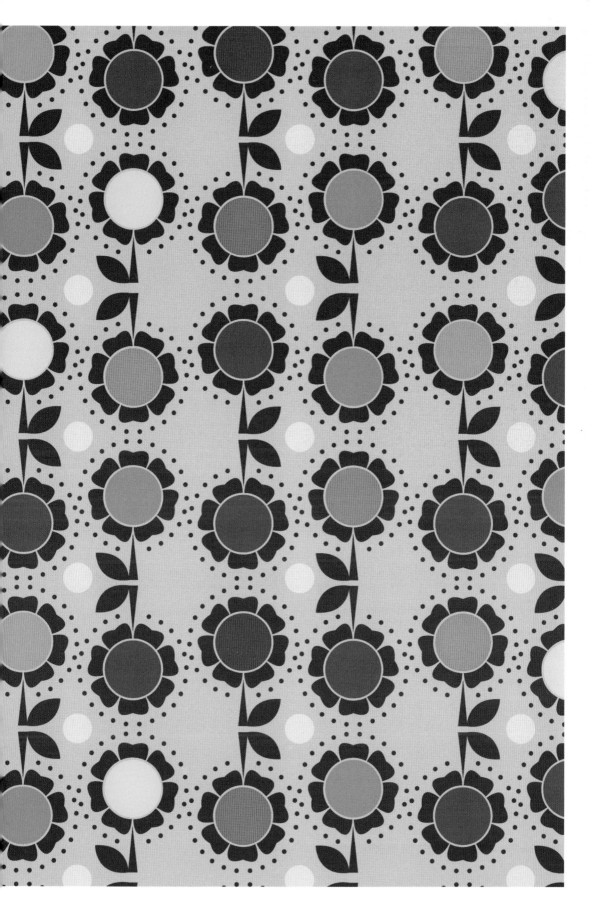

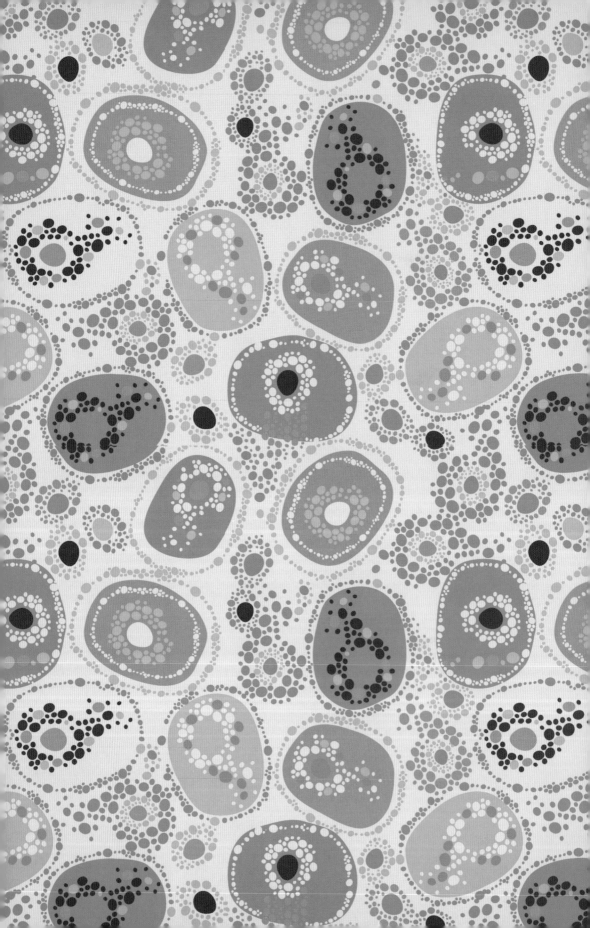

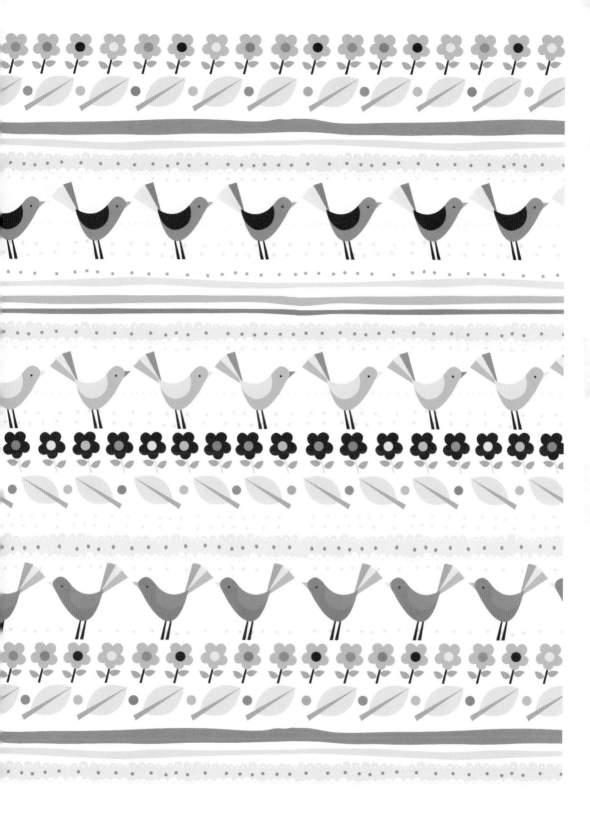

Opposite / Pebble Dots
Here Nicola was aiming for a more sophisticated look with an exploration into texture. When Nicola has created a design she will often print it off and crumple it to make little garment shapes and see how it would work as a fabric. 'This really brings it to life for me' she says.

Above / Folk Birds Pattern
Designed with an autumnal palette in mind, Nicola imagined this print to be used in some sort of kitchen design, either kitchen textiles or crockery. She felt it had movement with the little birds almost hopping along, even though it's based on a stripe concept.

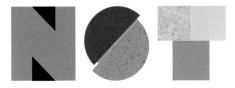

Nineteen Seventy Three

www.nineteenseventythree.com
enquiries@nineteenseventythree.com

73 // Nineteen Seventy Three are Emma and James Emmerson who established their paper product business in 2003. From their base in Brighton and Hove they publish a range of contemporary and environmentally friendly greeting cards. They publish artists including Eboy, Sanna Annuka, Jon Burgerman, Sukie, Darling Clementine, Catalina Estrada and Paul Thurlby. They also design their own collections and all the designs shown on these pages were created by James. Furthermore they have produced custom designs for clients including Sony BMG, Baltic Contemporary, Paperchase, and Oxfam.

Design Heroes:
Josef Muller Brockman, Andy Warhol, Peter Saville, Charley Harper.

All /
The Good Life series was designed by James Emmerson. His inspiration was a fusion of Scandinavian patterns and quirky characters with a simple, cool, wholesome feel. The studio uses paper made from 100% recycled waste for both the wrap and cards. The finished result is a fun, contemporary, eco-friendly range that appeals to adults as well as children.

73 / Nineteen Seventy Three

Noi Publishing

www.noipublishing.com
enquiries@noipublishing.com

74 // Noi Publishing are a family firm run by Tracy Francis and her husband Peter Francis together with his twin brother Paul Francis. Tracy does all the design work from their base in Farnham, Surrey. The trio were at college together in South Africa, where Tracy studied Graphic Design. She says they took a big leap of faith to become their own bosses and spend more time with their families. Tracy loves the fact that in design the trends are always changing and there is always a new colour combination or illustration style to get excited about and to give her own interpretation of. Fashion runway videos also offer Noi a source of inspiration from designers who revel in pattern and colour, and are brave, individual and funky.

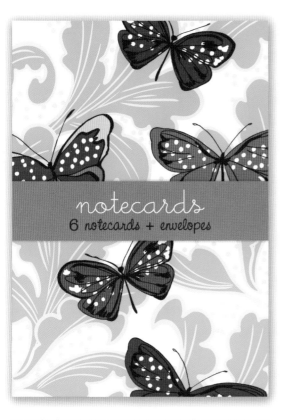

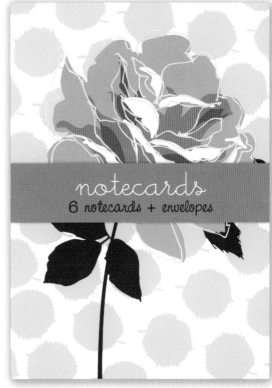

Opposite top /
New Home Card
From Noi's Sugar range, the
collection was printed with
a glitter finish that added a
lovely sparkle and texture.

Opposite bottom /
Thank You Notecards
Produced as a result of friends
and customers asking for
contemporary thank you
cards, this design has luscious
bright pink roses layered over
subtle grey spots.

Top / Notecards
Both taken from Noi's
Smile Range these colourful
notecards feature hand-drawn
blooms and butterflies.

Bottom / Birthday Card
Tracy hand draws most
of Noi's designs first before
colouring them on the
computer. This card draws
inspiration from the bright
colours and faceted cuts of
gemstones.

Owaboo

www.owaboo.co.uk
becky@owaboo.co.uk

75 // Becky Carr, the designer behind Owaboo, is originally from the North East of England and her company is named after her family dog Boo, ('Our Boo'). Becky studied Graphics and Illustration at Kingston Polytechnic and is now based in the Leicestershire countryside. Her first proper job was with Conran Design Group, and Terence Conran's belief that design should be a combination of function and form has stayed with her. When her designs sell well for customers she feels she has done her job properly. Becky has worked across all areas of fashion and tableware and has designed for George Davies, Gap, Next, WGSN and Marks & Spencer. She loves mid-century design, and is influenced by retro children's books and toys, Scandinavian design and Japanese children's design. As Becky says 'I'm never happier than when I'm designing. The idea that you can make something and sell it still really excites me.'

Design Heroes:
Saul Bass, Charley Harper, Paul Rand, Abner Graboff, Nineteen Seventy Three, Tim Hopgood.

Top / Happy Mice
Becky loves children's design and wanted to produce ranges that were 'kidult', appealing to both children and adults alike. Here she wanted the designs to have a nostalgic feel to them.

Bottom / Groovy Squirrel
From the Seventies range. Becky is of the generation who still draw on paper. She scans her images and works on them using Photoshop. Her designs have a retro feel to them, and she feels the quality of a hand-drawn line is different to line work produced solely on a computer.

Opposite / Birdies
From the Owaboo Birdy range of greeting cards. Becky wants the designs she produces to be commercial, but interesting. Her cards do well in galleries and design-led gift and bookshops.

Overleaf / Friendly Penguins & Curvy Butts
From the Owaboo Curvy Animals range of greetings cards that started life as textile designs and feature stylized animals and birds in repeat patterns.

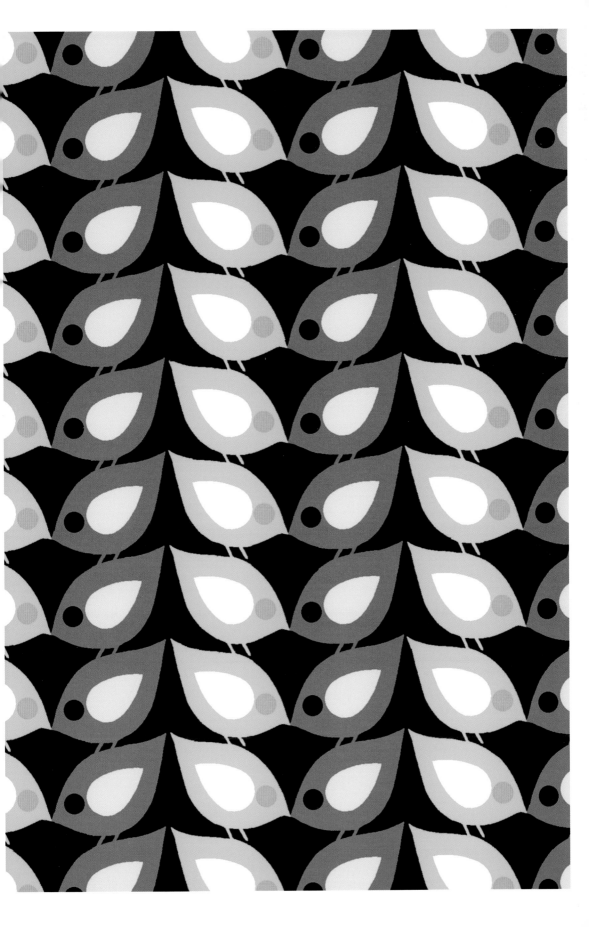

Paper & Cloth

www.paperandcloth.net
info@paperandcloth.net

76 // Paper & Cloth is a surface pattern design studio run by Jennie Rivers and based in Northampton. The studio promotes each of their designers under their own name as they passionately believe in showcasing talented designers to industry and allowing clients to be able to commission specific individuals. They have a real passion for hand-drawn illustration and love to create humorous and fun prints for kids, but they also specialize in beautiful hand-drawn details and textures for womenswear and tableware design. Another key influence in the studio's direction is a huge passion for vintage children's books. Clients have included Boden, John Lewis, Marks & Spencer, WH Smith, Macy's and Pottery Barn. They would now love to work with Habitat. Another ambition would be to use all of their artworks to decorate a children's play group.

Design Heroes:
Charley Harper, Delphine Durand, Olle Eksell.

Above / Once Upon A Time by Kate
Hand-drawn and then finished in Illustrator, this magical design was inspired by fantasy and paper cutting influences.

Opposite top left /
Forest Unicorn by Kate
A whimsical illustration featuring a magical fairy-tale forest and unicorns which was first hand-drawn and then finished in Illustrator.

Opposite top right /
Forest Friends by Yolande
Here the textured cross hatch background gives a contemporary feel and depth to the graphics and a nice contrast to the cute and whimsical creatures.

Opposite bottom / Tea Time by Kate
A simple and fun repeat using cutlery in different directions, created with kitchen textiles and tablewares in mind.

76 / Paper & Cloth

Opposite left / City Life by Yolande
This Paris themed design has a retro 1920s feel and uses hard lines for the cars for a naive handcut style.

Opposite right / Papercut Transport by Julia
Hand-drawn and edited in Photoshop. An increasing popularity with hand-cut and simple graphics in the children's market led to this simple bold design.

Above left / Doodle Square by Rachael
Hand-drawn and finished in Illustrator, these squares are filled with interest that cleverly look as though they could have been doodled thoughtlessly.

Above right / Folk Floral by Sarah
This design has a retro patchwork feel, inspired by the simple folk patterns that were so popular in the 1970s.

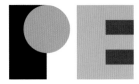

Patrick Edgeley

www.antigraphic.biz
patrick@antigraphic.biz

77 //   Patrick Edgeley studied Graphic Design in Richmond-upon-Thames and is currently based in Brighton and Hove. Patrick has been creating screen-prints for the last few years which he sells worldwide. Typography and Americana feature often in his work and he has been lucky enough to travel abroad to take inspiration. Patrick is also very interested in mid-century design, from textiles and advertising to architecture. Patrick's dream is to travel across America in a 1960s car drawing inspiration for his prints along the journey.

Design Heroes:
Saul Bass, Le Corbusier.

Above / Kitchen Utensils
Patrick's inspiration came from a large collection of kitchenalia that he has at home. Muted colours were used, reflecting the colours seen on many of the wooden handles.

Opposite / Retro Kitchen
This screen-print was inspired by his ever growing collection of retro kitchen ceramics and enamelware. All the items were hand-drawn and then screen-printed in a style that nods to the 1950s and '60s.

Patrick Hruby

www.patrickdrawsthings.com
www.friendandjohnson.com
patrickdrawsthings@gmail.com

78 // Patrick Hruby is originally from Spirit Lake in Idaho but is now based in Los Angeles. He studied Illustration at the Art Center College of Design in Pasadena where he was their Spring 2010 valedictorian. Patrick finds inspiration for his work from nature, Disneyland and vintage children's books. He has a talent for mathematics and often uses geometry in his work to bold effect. Since graduating he has been much in demand from clients such as AMMO Books, Todd Oldham, New York Times Magazine, NoBrow and Fishs Eddy. Patrick has also been included in the CMYK Top 100 New Creatives list. His next aim is to design wallpaper and textiles.

Design Heroes:
Charley Harper, Mary Blair, Paul Rand, Alexander Girard, Kay Neilsen.

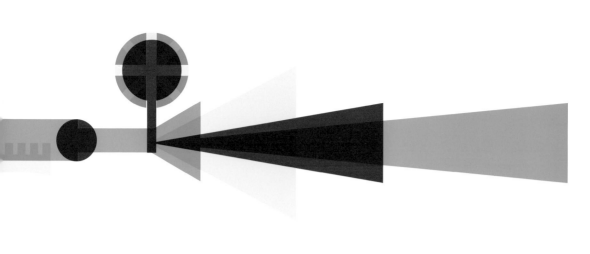

Top / Ray Gun
Patrick wanted to make a piece about the toys he had whilst growing up and has used a striking CMYK colour palette.

Bottom left / Ice Flower
All of the works featured were created by Patrick using Adobe Illustrator and on this one – inspired by a flower Patrick found growing in the snow – he creates recognizable organic forms out of mathematical geometry.

Bottom right / Twins
Striking flowers in mirror image were created for a zine a friend of Patrick's was putting together about families and family relationships.

Opposite / Fish Of The Sea
This stunning multicoloured fish made of sharp angles and
smooth arcs was inspired by the Brothers Grimm story
The Fisherman's Wife.

Above / Dream Buildings
Patrick wanted to create a fun image, inspired by his love of
fairy tales, that was as interesting upside-down as it was upright.

Petit Collage

www.petitcollage.com
www.lorenasiminovich.com
info@petitcollage.com

79 // Lorena Siminovich studied graphic design in Buenos Aires in her native Argentina, but is now based in San Francisco. Lorena splits her time between her company Petit Collage and her career as a children's book writer and illustrator. Lorena's clients have included Chronicle Books, Pottery Barn, Galison, and Anthropologie. Influences on her work are drawn from a love of Scandinavian design, mid-century design and vintage children's books.

Design Heroes :
Alexander Girard, Charley Harper, Mary Blair, Olle Eksel, Paul Rand, Bruno Munari.

Top /
Mushroom Collage on Wood
A handmade collage on FSC-certified maple plywood featuring papers collected from Lorena's travels from all over the world. Created as a limited edition of 50 for Petit Collage where no two are exactly alike in texture or pattern.

Bottom / Red Bird Trio
This strikingly simple arrangement of birds is a handmade collage on FSC-certified maple plywood created for Petit Collage.

Top /
Petit Collage Notecards: Owl,
Rabbit & Squirrel
Lorena has illustrated a
series of designs published
by Chronicle Books. The
highly detailed designs are
full of interesting textures
and belong to a box set
of stationery. They are
made from 100% recycled
paper and soy inks and are
contained in a beautiful
keepsake box.

Bottom left / It Takes
A Village Print on Wood
Illustrated by Lorena
especially for Petit Collage,
this whimsical architecture
was printed on sustainably
grown, chemical-free maple
veneer.

Bottom right /
New York Print on Wood
New York's skyline has been
printed onto sustainably
grown, chemical-free maple
veneer as part of a city series
of places Lorena has lived in.

Pintuck

www.pintuck.co.uk
www.maryfellowsprints.co.uk
mary@maryfellows.co.uk

80 // Pintuck is the work of designer Mary Fellows who runs her company from Lewes, East Sussex. Mary studied for a 3D Design degree at Manchester Polytechnic as well as a master's degree in Design at the University of Brighton. Mary is influenced most by mid-century design and packaging and loves to include retro adages in her work which still resonate strongly today. Pintuck products include tea towels, tote bags and aprons which are all designed, printed and sewn in England. Mary has also created a Pintuck range of mugs with McLaggan Smith and a range of cards published by Nineteen Seventy Three. She would now love to branch out into food packaging.

Design Hero:
Tom Eckersley.

Top / Make Do And Mend
A British wartime slogan
is revived and brought bang
up-to-date by Pintuck.
The design has a three-
dimensional quality to the
type and an interesting detail
is provided by the pinking
shears shaped border.

Bottom / Happy Ending
Mary loves to work with
typography and slogans.
By experimenting with fonts
and scale she has created a
striking design.

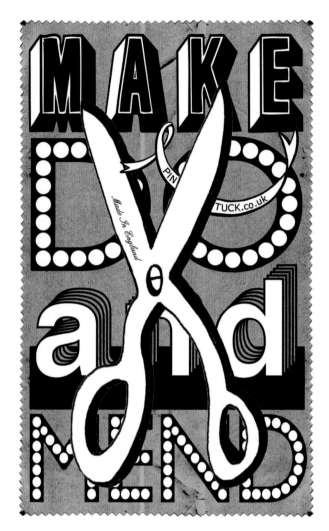

Top / Beautiful Day
A retro design created for a tea towel where Mary has obviously enjoyed playing with the type to create a bright and breezy layout.

Bottom / Apple A Day
This classic slogan is illustrated in a big and bold design featuring decorative typography for use on tea towels and prints.

Prints Charming

www.printscharming.com.au
www.printscharming.typepad.com
info@printscharming.com.au

81 //   Prints Charming is a fabric design studio located in Sydney, Australia created by Cath Derksema and Kirsten Junor. Cath has a degree majoring in textiles from Edith Cowan University in Western Australia and Kirsten studied costumes at the National Institute of Dramatic Art in Sydney. The duo design fabric prints for clients such as FreeSpirit and Marcus Fabrics, and run workshops in sewing and screen-printing to teach their skills to others. Their first book *Prints Charming* was published in May 2010 by Murdoch Books. For inspiration, Kirsten is influenced by clothing and fabrics from the past and different cultures. Cath likes an eclectic 1970s craft box and both admire Marimekko. Prints Charming, they say, 'is all about modern contemporary craft, to inspire and excite'. One of their future ambitions is to take their classes worldwide.

Design Heroes:
Too many to mention – everyone from Matisse to Citroën.

Above / Cars & Trees
Designed for a fabric range, the artwork was screen-printed using a paper cut method of printing. The result is a contemporary children's fabric that is colourful and whimsical.

Opposite / Rainbow Garden
This print is influenced by the wonderfully illustrated children's books of the 1970s. The original art work was screen-printed using a paper cut method of printing. The bright translucent colours reflect the bright Australian light.

Rachel Cave

www.rachelcave.co.uk
rachelcavedesign.blogspot.com
rachelcave1@hotmail.com

82 // Rachel Cave is originally from Wiltshire but now lives in London after taking a degree in Surface Design at the London College of Communication. Rachel's bold graphic patterns have won her commissions from clients such as Tigerprint, Typhoon, Joseph Joseph, Jenny Duff and Creative Tops. Her main influences are from 1950s and '60s design and Scandinavian retro. Rachel is also represented by Lemon Ribbon where she sells her prints all over the world. One day she would love to create her own line of products.

Design Heroes:
Marianne Westman, Lucienne Day, Orla Kiely.

Top / Midnight Trees
An atmospheric print comprising hand-drawn trees with a folk Scandinavian influence designed for Rachel's personal portfolio.

Bottom / Dotty Floral
Here Rachel's flowers have been distilled down to the very essence that is needed to make them still recognizable as a flower. Created for her personal portfolio.

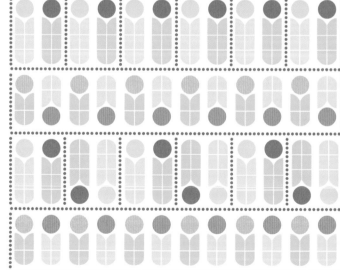

Top / Pop Floral
A retro floral print designed for interiors. The stylized flowers have radiating centres and an interesting textural feel with the cross hatching contained in the strong leaf shapes.

Bottom / Apples & Pears
A fruit pattern that was designed for Rachel's personal portfolio. Her work often has a strong graphic element with clean lines. The addition of the flower shapes adds interest and softens the look.

Rebecca Elfast

www.rebelform.se
www.rebeccaelfast.com
info@rebelform.se

83 // Rebecca Elfast is based in Gothenburg, Sweden. She has always drawn and painted in her spare time, alongside studying architecture for five years. Rebecca is now running her own little company, doing what she loves most: painting, drawing and designing. She enjoys taking on very different assignments and challenging herself every day. Clients have included architecture firms, ad agencies, magazines and home textile companies. Rebecca finds that everything can be an inspiration if you're in the right frame of mind, but that it is especially true of nature, people, travel, everyday situations, music and books.

Above / Falling Leaves
This design started out as multiple pen sketches that were digitally arranged into a dense whirlwind of autumn leaves. Rebecca wanted something to suit a textile feel so this could be suitable for fabrics, pillows or curtains.

Opposite top left / Tiny Flowers
Tiny tulip-like flowers arranged in half-circles form this über-cute, sugar sweet pattern. It would be perfect for gift wrap, textiles or baby clothes.

Opposite top right / Seed Pods
A hand-drawn/digital seamless vector pattern of delicate botanical studies, largely in outline only.

Opposite bottom left / Coral
A seamless vector pattern for textile or paper with a 1950s retro feel. Coral-like, marine shapes are heavily stacked on top of one another with dots, ovals and juicy colours.

Opposite bottom right / City
Created with wallpaper in mind so you can have a big city covering an entire wall. Available from Studio Nommo.

Rob Ryan

www.misterrob.co.uk

84 // Rob Ryan was born in Cyprus to Irish parents. He now lives in London where he has worked as an artist and illustrator since graduating from The Royal College of Art with a master's degree in printmaking. Rob is best known for his beautiful and intricate paper cuts which have a thoughtful, romantic and whimsical feel, but he also works with screen-printing to create artworks, ceramics and greeting cards. Rob recently created a licensed collection with Wild & Wolf to expand his works onto a wider variety of products. Besides his own projects Rob has also worked with many clients including Paul Smith, Fortnum & Mason, Liberty and Urban Outfitters. In 2008 Rob opened Ryantown a shop in London's Columbia Road inspired by the artist Keith Haring's New York store in the 1980s, with the idea of making his work available to everyone. This is further reinforced by his online Etsy shop Mister Rob. Publications include a book of his artworks entitled *This Is For You*. His dream commission would be to design a 'really really brilliant tree house!'

Design Heroes:
Titian, Raphael, Caspar David Friedrich.

Top / Please Drink
A screen-printed tile design that was later applied to a water bottle by Wild & Wolf.

Bottom / Every Beat
A screen-printed tile design featuring birds framed by a chained necklace that ingeniously incorporates the type.

Above / Bird Lady
Working silhouettes gave Rob
the chance to worry less about
the detailing of the image and
more about the soul of the
picture. This screen-printed
lady is beautifully framed in
a decorative illustrated border.

Top /
Rob Ryan Wild & Wolf Selection
Demand for Rob's products has always
been greater than his time could allow
but he was always reluctant to allow mass
manufacturing of his product. Thankfully
a close friend of Rob's at Wild & Wolf
was able to ensure he could still have full
control over the design and quality.

Bottom / Other Planets
A two colour screen-print in sand and
green where two birds are holding up a
nest of eggs. The emotive and moving
text reads 'Other planets cannot be as
beautiful as this one.'

Opposite top / Bunting

Left top / Listen Mug
With all his work Rob likes to focus on the emotional content and the sayings used, such as 'listen to the world'. Produced for Wild & Wolf who allowed Rob to be involved in the details such as the cut out lettering on the box.

Left middle / Vase
'Please smell us' is the delightful slogan on this flower vase. The striking blues of the silhouettes looks fresh and is followed through onto the equally beautiful packaging.

Left bottom / Other Planets Plate
A perfect example of how Rob's designs can transfer onto products. The tree perfectly sits within the well of the plate and the co-ordinating box is minimal yet strongly branded. For Wild & Wolf.

Below / Canvas Shopper

Robin Zingone

www.robinzingone.com
www.robinzingone.blogspot.com

85 // Robin Zingone is originally from New York, but now calls Connecticut home. She attended Parsons School of Design in New York, majoring in Illustration, and then worked in the editorial and advertising field illustrating for clients such as Microsoft, *New York Times*, American Express, *Vanity Fair*, and *Better Homes and Gardens*. Currently Robin is a licensor and works with a whole new set of clients, including Mattel, Papyrus, Hallmark, and Skinit to name just a few. She can find inspiration anywhere from an electric blue Eero Saarinen chair, to a golden cat curled up on a tomato-red sofa, or bright yellow taxis speeding down Park Avenue. She is also inspired by the Print & Pattern blog.

Design Heroes:
Matisse, Paul Rand, Jim Flora, David Hockney, Richard Avedon, Rex Ray, Stuart Davis, Kirsten Ulve.

Right / Growth/Song
From the Life Is Beautiful collection. Sadly in 2008, Robin's brain started to bleed from a rare birth defect. After having five mini strokes and, ultimately, brain surgery, she began to slowly recover and these were the first images she drew. Robin based them on the simplest joys of life: warmth, contentment, happiness and beauty. The collection can be seen on custom art prints.

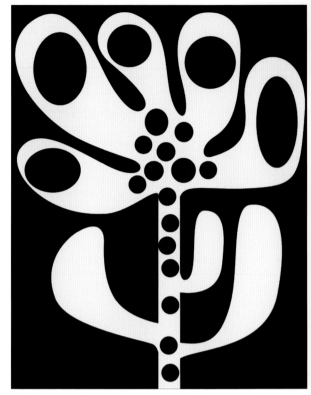

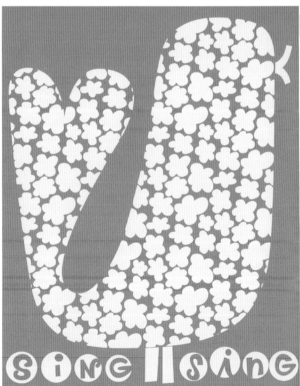

Top / Fab Flower
This print is part of Robin's Girlygirl™ brand. Based on a fabulous fashionista, who is one part princess and one part rockstar. She wanted to use strong jewel tones and bold shapes to blend with her personality.

Bottom / Lollapalooza/Zinnia/Allium
From Robin's Flowerchild collection. Based on a Japanese cute *kawaii* idea, with 'a bit of Palm Beach preppy thrown in'. The colours are fun, flirty and happy, and the white graphics give them a modern feel. Robin's licensees are currently using them for greeting cards, stationery, journals, custom art prints and as skins for electronic devices.

Roddy & Ginger

www.roddyandginger.co.uk
virginia@roddyandginger.co.uk

86 // Virginia Armstrong is based in London where in 2008 she set up a screen-printing workshop in her studio to hand-print her designs in small batches onto cotton and linen. She sells her products through her small company Roddy & Ginger both online and in a small selection of shops. Previously, Virginia studied graphic design in Canterbury and worked for many years as a packaging and print designer for a number of London design consultancies. She now works as a freelance graphic and textile designer and loves to create designs that are cheerful, colourful and uplifting! Her plan is to bring out a couple of new collections each year and her inspiration comes from a mix of vintage children's book illustrations, folk art, Scandinavian and retro textile designs, and ceramics – all of which she collects avidly!

Top / Happy Birds Olive
Influenced by the simplicity of Scandinavian design in a traditional folk-style layout.

Bottom left / Daisy Bird & City Windows
A selection of Roddy & Ginger's hand-printed linen cushions photographed by Heather Lewin.

Bottom right /
Happy Birds Cushion On Chair
All of Virginia's cushions are hand screen-printed onto natural linen and handmade. Beautifully photographed here by Heather Lewin.

Top / Love Hearts
Two love birds created
as a screen-print for
romantic occasions such as
Valentine's Day or weddings.
The wonderful muted colours
give it a retro folk flavour.

Middle left / Daisy Bird
A beautiful graphic
Scandinavian inspired
bird which can be found
on cushions, aprons and
art prints.

Middle right /
Roddy & Ginger
Two owl characters with
a mid-century modern feel,
designed as a logo for the
Roddy & Ginger brand
and developed further for
a stylish screen-print.

Bottom / Daisy Pattern
A simple but effective
geometric floral print that
was designed as the perfect
complement for the *Daisy
Bird* design. Often used as
co-ordinating fabric for use
on the back of cushions.

Rosie Wonders

www.rosiewonders.co.uk
shop.rosiewonders.co.uk
rosie@rosiewonders.co.uk

87 // Rosie Wonders is based in Hackney in London where she creates greeting cards and jewellery from her studio. Rosie studied Broadcasting but gave up her career working in television as she wanted to be more creative. She taught herself Photoshop and the business has grown from there. Rosie is inspired by travel and vintage items – this comes from her mum and aunt who are both artists and great collectors. If she has an idea, Rosie tends to do some research and then put it in an ideas/development folder. Then when she has time to design she'll go back to the folder and pick out what grabs her. 'I don't like to follow trends' Rosie says, 'I focus mainly on drawing vintage objects and like to find strange little characters or figurines to feature in my work.'

Design Heroes:
Edward Gorey, Henry Darger.

Top / Pop Boy & Girl
Created from a drawing of some figurines
Rosie found on Ebay.

Bottom / Beaded Lovebirds Wedding Card
Rosie likes eclectic mixes of images and mediums and tends to collect little shapes and sketches to use at a later date. The birds are surrounded by flower confetti and the finished card is embellished with pink glitter dots and a jewel.

Top left / Pennysylvania Dutch 'Distelfink'
The idea for this range came from the Amish people of Pennsylvania who often decorate their wooden furniture with folk images of birds and tulips and images of wedded bliss.

Top right / Blossom Bird Card
Of over 300 designs, this is Rosie's most popular card design. Rosie used a photograph of her boyfriend's mother's garden in the Lake District but added a little bird and some glitter to make it just right.

Bottom left / Pennysylvania Dutch Chicks
Taken from a range that took a year to design, Rosie just couldn't get them right until she thought to put a wooden background behind the bright sketches.

Bottom right / Stone Birds Card
Rosie's images, such as these cute birds, are hand-drawn, scanned and then finished in Photoshop. The cards are then handmade, often using glitter, beads and jewels.

Ruth Green

www.ruthgreendesign.com
www.ruthgreendesign@hotmail.com

88 // Ruth Green studied first for a degree in Textile Design at Liverpool John Moores University, followed by a master's in Textile Printing at U.C.E. Birmingham. Now from her studio in Kings Heath, just south of Birmingham city centre, she produces a variety of screen-prints, etchings and lino cuts. Ruth is a big fan of mid-century design, especially Scandinavian ceramics from the 1960s and '70s. She also finds that the process of printing sparks new ideas continuously. Clients have included IKEA, Te Neues, The Art Group, Art Print Japan, and Cardmix. Most recently she worked with Tate Publishing on a children's book.

Design Heroes:
Angie Lewin, Rob Ryan, Orla Kiely, Tim Biskup, Lucienne Day, Pete Fowler, Marc Boutavant, Stig Lindberg, Bjorn Wiinblad, Sanna Annuka.

Top / Springtime
The red version, Ladybirds, appeared in *Elle Decoration* magazine in February 2008. The plain shape of the tree contrasts perfectly with all the detailing of the branches.

Bottom / Leaf & Stone
Ruth finds inspiration in all sorts of places such as a pebble found on a beach. In this screen-print the pebble is kept flat and simple while the detail comes from using a different shaped stalk in each leaf.

Top left / Rosa
All of the designs featured were created for Ruth's personal portfolio. This screen-print from an original drawing was from an edition of 50.

Top right / Dicky Bird
Screen-print from original drawing, edition of 70. Published by IKEA for their 'Tvilling' art print range in 2009.

Bottom left / Comice
Screen-print from an original drawing of a flower-filled pear, this was produced as a limited edition of 32.

Bottom right / Pink Pippin
Screen-print from original drawing, this delicious apple was produced as an edition of 50. Published by TeNeues in 2010 (with green background) as Botanica notecard packs.

Sally Boyle

www.sallyboyle.co.uk
sally@sallyboyle.co.uk

89 // Sally Boyle is based in Yorkshire. She is a self-taught designer who studied English at university and then moved from magazine design/sub-editing into freelance graphic design. Sally is inspired by Ronald Searle, Lotte Reiniger, Kay Neilson and traditional fairy tale illustration. Her work features influences from folk design and from Scandinavian, Japanese and Eastern European design. Clients have included greeting cards and stationery companies in Britain and America, several national magazines and travel guide publishers. Sally says of her work process 'I create all my prints in the same way: I write a list of associated elements I might want to include, search Google for relevant photos, scribble some appalling sketches and then create the components in Illustrator, shuffling them about like fuzzy felts until I have a little scene.' Her dream commission would be to design a film set for Terry Gilliam (or another film director of that ilk).

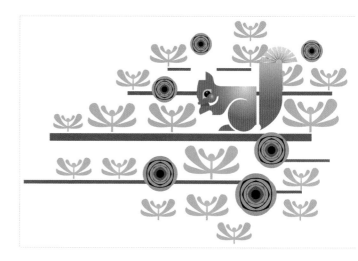

Top & bottom / Meadow: Spring & Red Squirrel: Autumn
From a printable card set designed by Sally and inspired by seasonal change. Her work features folkloric motifs and fairy-tale inspired scenes.

Opposite / Horse Chestnut
This design was created for a printable card set available on Etsy. As you can see from this stylized tree Sally is 'obsessed with creating the perfect, near geometric form.'

Opposite / Owl: Winter
From the same printable card set inspired by seasonal change as *Meadow: Spring & Red Squirrel*.

Top / Birdhouse
Sally uses geometric forms to illustrate her motifs and builds up a scene piece by piece. The result is something very unique.

Bottom / Indian Peacock
This striking peacock, as with lots of Sally's work, uses 'gradients' of colour blending from one shade to another.

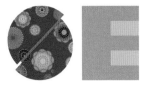

Sally Elford

www.sallyelford.co.uk

90 // Sally Elford has been based in Brighton ever since she graduated with a degree in Illustration from Brighton University. Now working as an illustrator, designer and printmaker Sally is inspired by mid-century art, Art Deco, Scandinavian style decorations and the stylized floral and foliage shapes found in nature. She will often find inspiration from an image with pleasing colour combinations which can be used as a starting point. Sally's clients have included Asda/Wallmart, The Victoria and Albert Museum and teNeues.

Design Heroes:
Lucienne Day, Helen Dardik, Mibo, Sanna Annukka, Fiona Howard, the Provensens.

Top / Modern Blossom Here Sally experiments with different colourways for her Art Deco inspired Spring design.

Bottom / Deco Floral Stylized simple geometric shapes and muted colours have been used in this busy all over pattern created with stationery and furnishing fabrics in mind.

Above / Floral 1
Derived from the original
In Full Bloom image these
variations use the same limited
colour palette.

Left / In Full Bloom
Designed with a screen-print
in mind Sally has created a tall
elegant piece featuring graphic
blooms in a variety of shapes
and sizes.

Sanderson

www.sanderson-uk.com
enquiries@a-sanderson.co.uk

91 // Founded by Arthur Sanderson in 1860, Sanderson is an internationally renowned brand in the field of interior design and decorating. Its quintessentially English fabrics and wallpapers, bedlinen, paint and tableware collections offer classic, inspirational products, design innovation and exceptional quality. Well-known for its traditional, English-inspired design, Sanderson is also innovative in its use of colour and production techniques. The company draws on the creativity of young contemporary designers, alongside the work of artists and historical documents. This mix creates new and leading designs for modern living. The Sanderson design archive houses one of the largest collections of fabrics, wallpaper and printing blocks in the world with samples dating back to the Renaissance. This resource is a constant inspiration to the design studio, which is always looking at new ways of re-interpreting these design classics to suit modern tastes.

Right / Dandelion Clocks
Colour: Chaffinch.
Designed by Fiona Howard for Sanderson, this stunning mid-century inspired design features beautiful stylized dandelion seed heads, capturing a retro flavour.

Far right / Dandelion Clocks
Colour: Blackcurrant.
Designed by Fiona Howard for Sanderson, this beautiful 1950s-style print was such a huge hit as fabrics and wallpapers that it also made it onto ceramics and bed-linen.

Sassafras

www.sassafraslass.com
www.sassafras.typepad.com
graphics@sassafraslass.com

92 // Sassafras is currently based on the central coast of California at San Luis Obispo. Founded by Tim and Rebecca McAllister the company has been established for seven years. They started out in scrapbooking but have expanded to create a broad range of paper crafting offering much more than the 'typical scrapbook page'. Their inspiration and trend research comes from all over but mainly from children's clothing, children's books, interior design, advertising and vintage thrift shopping. All of the designs featured here are by Tim McAllister for Sassafras. Sassafras aim to continue designing products that stretch creative boundaries. Its dream is to take the company's style far beyond the pages of your scrapbook to textiles, children's books, animation and beyond.

Above / Love To Learn
Delightful cutesy characters are mixed with bold retro numbers from the Count Me In collection inspired by the idea of elementary learning.

Opposite top / One Thru Twelve
Tim has a wonderful understanding of typography and a flair for making his work look like found vintage pieces while keeping it strikingly current and fashionable.

Opposite middle /
Nerdy Bird Sweet Treats
All of Tim's designs for Sassafras are created using both Illustrator and Photoshop, and he works in two styles – one having a whimsical feel, the other a collaged vintage feel to create a 'found' look. Nerdy Bird fits into the former with its delightful cutesy characters.

Opposite bottom / Tailored Deck
More great typography from Tim, only this time using the concept of stitching and fabrics.

Silvia Dekker

www.silviadekker.nl
www.lillarogers.com
info@lillarogers.com

93 // Silvia Dekker grew up in a small village in the middle of the Dutch flower district. After receiving a degree in Conceptual Art and Design at the Royal Academy of Art in The Hague in 1997, Silvia studied Fashion and Textile Design. Silvia now lives in the city of Leiden with her partner and two sons, Felix and Silvester. She started working as a freelance illustrator and surface pattern designer in 2001 and her main client is Dutch department store HEMA, which has over 500 stores in Europe. She first started designing prints for HEMA's baby and childrenswear collections and now each year she also designs postcards, tablewares, bedding, 'back to school' stationery and Christmas cards for the store. Silvia has been represented by Lilla Rogers Studio since September 2009 and her work is available for licensing and commissions from the studio. Her designs have been used to produce a range of fabric in the United States, and she has worked on projects for murals and a scrapbooking line. In the future Silvia would love to work in Japan.

Top / Best Friends
From a collection of six children's postcards created for HEMA. Two cute characters are brought to life by Silvia's delicate use of pattern fills.

Bottom / Easter Plate & Mug
Dutch department store HEMA designed an Easter plate and mug using Silvia's folk motif illustrations.

Above / Pop Flowers
Silvia designed this as a personal piece available for licensing.
Colourful tall blooms are full of different interesting shapes.

Above / Pink & Green Flower Branches
Created in Illustrator for HEMA babywear. Very little detail
is needed on the flowers as the silhouette shapes speak for
themselves.

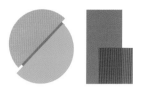

Sol Linero

www.sollinero.com
www.sollinero.etsy.com
sol@sollinero.com

94 //   Sol Linero is based in Buenos Aires, where she studied Graphic Design at the unversity. She now works as an illustrator, animator and designer. Her inspirations come from everything that surrounds her, from furniture and food, to the weather, buildings, flowers, trees and her beloved dog Poncho. As she works at home most of the time, her pets are her loyal friends and company throughout the day. Sol's design influences are all things vintage and retro. She loves going to flea markets, and spending hours searching for vintage books. Sol is also a huge fan of Russian graphic design, mid-century design, animation, Cubism and retro futurism. She is represented by The Loud Cloud. In the future she would love to design a window display for Anthropologie, and a dinnerware set or a children's book.

Design Heroes:
Mary Blair, Charley Harper,
Marc Boutavant, Olle Eksel.

Top / Etsy Banner
This was designed for Sol's Etsy shop and was created in Illustrator. She wanted to represent herself as a designer and illustrator, so tried to include things that are cute, retro and fun.

Above / Castillo
This piece was created as an extension of the poster ABC. Sol loved how the individual letters came out so she decided to do them as separate posters.

Top / Sol Linero Logo
Created for Sol's web page, she wanted to make it feel part of the entire site design, and not just a traditional logo at the top of the web page. She also tried to give it a handmade feel by adding texture.

Bottom left /
Poncho Y Lupita
This illustration was created as a *giclée* print for a French online gallery. It was digitally made in Illustrator and Sol added the shadowing in Photoshop afterwards.

Bottom right / Tea Cups
This was a personal Gocco print for an exhibition whose theme was 'tea time'. It was a really happy experience for Sol, giving her the opportunity to find her own personal style.

Solitaire

www. solitaireshop.com
studio@solitaireshop.com

95 // Solitaire is the work of husband-and-wife team Matt and Em Bruty who are both from Essex and based in Leigh-on-Sea. Matt studied Illustration at Central St Martins in London and Em studied Fashion and Printed Textiles at the University of the West of England. Their designs are inspired by 'the eccentricities of English tradition, British birds and wildlife, vintage crockery, childhood nostalgia, living by the seaside and the love of drinking tea.' In 2008 Solitaire won 'Most on trend product' at the Top Drawer exhibition, and their place mats were voted best product in 2009 at the House & Garden Style Awards in Australia. Their products are sold by a variety of stockists including Anthropologie, the Victoria and Albert Museum, the Barbican, and To Dry For. They absolutely love what they do and their only ambition is just to keep on doing it.

Design Heroes:
Matt – Robert Gilmore,
Em – Liberty print designs.

Above / Always Time For Tea
All of Solitaire's products are screen-printed with water based inks and are all British-made and supplied. This is a hand-drawn illustration of a decorative teapot where the type has been beautifully worked into a plume of steam.

Top left / Tea Cup Pocket Apron
Featuring a hand-drawn illustration of a vintage teacup decorated
with hearts and birds, which is in fact a secret pocket.

Top right / Tea Pot Pocket Apron
Inspired by Em's love of vintage crockery this hand-drawn illustration
of a stylish antique teapot is hand-printed onto 100% cotton.

Bottom left / Yay! Cake Card
A single hand-drawn cupcake looks very special in the centre of this
hand-printed card. Placed on a lace doily with typography made from
sugar sprinkles.

Bottom right / Birthday Cake Card
A nostalgic hand-drawn cake using a simple colour palette has been
lovingly screen-printed onto 100% recycled card.

Soul

www.souluk.com
smile@souluk.com

96 // Soul is a card publishing company based in Oxford, which was founded by David Hicks in 1997. Its wide variety of cards are sold internationally, but mostly in the United Kingdom to boutique card and gift shops. Soul has in-house designers as well as using freelance artists to get a really diverse mix. It takes inspiration from all aspects of design (interiors, tablewares, fine art, graphics etc.) and tries to keep up-to-date with the latest trends as well as starting some of its own! Besides greeting cards, Soul also produces a number of stationery items, notebooks and gift wrap. It has won numerous awards and has a sister company that produces cards called Really Good.

Top / Oasis by Vicki Aust Greeting card created in Illustrator featuring a pattern filled tree and heart set off with a flourish and two highly stylized birds, finished with coloured foil.

Bottom / Frappe by Vicki Aust Greeting card created in Photoshop. The bold hand-drawn style type is finished with silver foil and flitter.

Top left / Happiness 1
by Emma Davis
Greeting card. A vase of
coloured dots form a stylized
bunch of flowers in this
mixed media collage which
was assembled in Photoshop
and finished with silver foil
and flitter.

Top right /
Happiness Wrap 2
by Emma Davis
Wrapping paper featuring
a photomontage of stylish
retro ceramics, finished with
silver foil.

Middle left / Glace
by Vicki Aust
Greeting card created in
Illustrator. A fun elephant
is topped off with a speech
bubble of lively type and
finished with coloured foil.

Middle right / Oasis Wrap
by Vicki Aust
Wrapping paper featuring
a bold all-over print of
simplified trees that are
layered to give depth. Created
in Illustrator and finished
with coloured foil.

Bottom left / Happiness 3
by Emma Davis
Greeting card with a hand
cut look to the leaves and
tree trunk created as a collage
assembled in Photoshop and
finished with silver foil and
flitter.

Bottom right / Juice
Greeting card created in
Illustrator featuring bright
rings of spots, stripes, and
checks, finished with silver
foil and flitter.

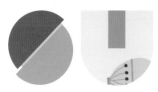

Suzy Ultman

www.lillarogers.com/artists/suzy-ultman
www.etsy.com/shop/suzyultman

97 // Suzy Ultman is from Pennsylvania but is now located in Columbus, Ohio. Suzy draws her inspiration from childhood memories. As a child she spent her time collecting stickers, playing board games, perfecting her Snoopy sketches, woodworking with her father and baking with her mother. Suzy says 'That girl is present every time I draw.' She has always been very nostalgic and loves to spend hours at flea markets or antique malls searching for visual inspiration. She is also inspired by travel and has a long list of design heroes. Suzy is represented by the fabulous Lilla Rogers and clients have included Crate & Barrel, Madison Park Greetings and Robert Kaufman Fabrics.

Design Heroes:
Mary Blair, Dick Bruna, Paul Rand, Charles Schultz, Yoshitomo Nara, Marc Jacobs, Fiep Westendorp.

Top / Masha and Friends From Masha and Friends Notecards, published by Chronicle Books. This set was inspired by Russian folk art, but the soul of the project comes from her childhood when she spent years collecting dolls from around the world.

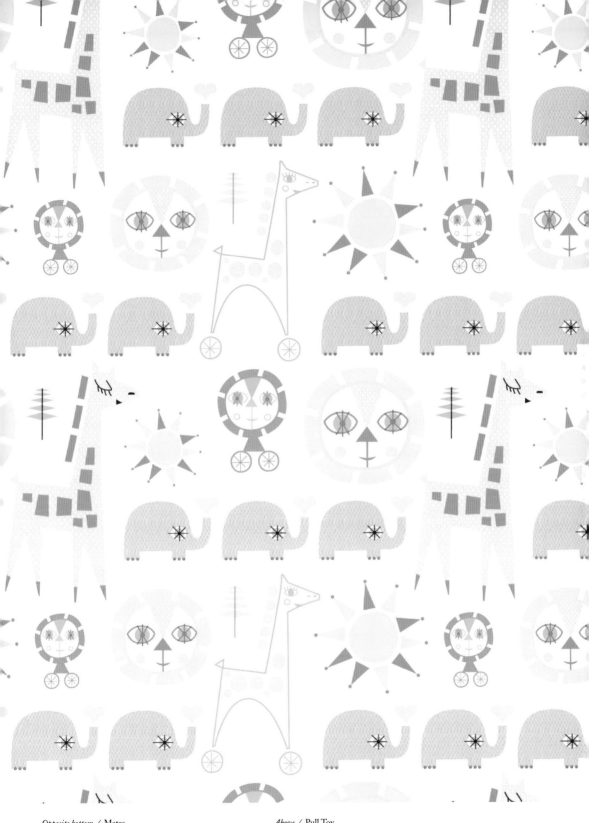

Top left /
Paper Doll Parade Jilly
From Paper Doll Parade,
published by Chronicle Books.
Based on Suzy's dear friend
Jilly. She has wonderfully
original ways of illustrating
eyes in many of her works.

Top right / Give A Hoot
From Home Sweet Home
Decorative Prints, published
by Chronicle Books. The
series is based on Suzy's time
in New England. In this print
no two owls are the same.

Bottom / Paper Doll Parade
From Paper Doll Parade,
published by Chronicle
Books. Every doll is based on
someone in Suzy's life. This
design demonstrates perfectly
her wonderful use of textures
and fills.

Above / Just Right
From Home Sweet Home Decorative Prints, published by
Chronicle Books. For Suzy this piece was about finding that
place where life feels safe and cosy. The textured background
gives it a sense of warmth by taking away any starkness.

Team Kitten

www.teamkitten.com
www.teamkitten.com/blog
kat@teamkitten.com

98 //   Kat Cameron is the designer behind Team Kitten and is based on Australia's Gold Coast. Kat has been designing and creating for over ten years as a textile designer, pattern maker and illustrator. She describes her style as Japanese *kawaii* influenced by a folk Scandinavian twist. Kat has two small children, Tyler and Juniper, and her partner is another creative, Josh Thorsen. Clients have included Coca-Cola, Emirates Airlines, Puffin Books, Cadbury and Mambo. She also licences Team Kitten prints onto products such as gift wrap, wall stickers and mugs.

Design Heroes:
Junko Mizuno, Orla Kiely, Decole, Shinzi Katoh.

Above / Forest New
Striking tree shapes are staggered in repeat with bands of colours.

Opposite / Wonderfalls Pattern
This repeat pattern came from using Team Kitten's iconic squirrel and other folksy images Kat loves. She wanted to convey a 'wonderful waterfall' of graphics. This design has been made into wrapping paper and wellies.

Overleaf left / Babooshka Pattern
Created as an accompaniment pattern design for Kat's matryoshka collection of wall art stickers which was featured as part of a designer collection by Team Kitten.

Overleaf right / I Heart Tea
Repeat pattern for gift wrap paper and stationery, based on Kat's love of drinking tea and cute *kawaii* faces. This has since been made into wallpaper.

Valentina Ramos

www.valentinaramos.com
www.valentinadesign.etsy.com
valentina_ramos@yahoo.com

99 //   Valentina Ramos is originally from Venezuela but now lives in Miami. She graduated with a degree in Graphic Design in 1994 from the Centro Artistico Villasmil de Leon in Venezuela. Valentina is part of the design team at Pink Light Design and creates her own prints, paintings and drawings for sale on Etsy. She is always inspired by artwork with intricate details, and pointillism had a big influence on her during her formative years. Valentina says 'I try to bring a fantastical, dreamlike appearance to my artwork.' She would love to see her designs applied across different products, like the Vera Bradley range.

Design Heroes:
Charley Harper, Johanna Basford.

Above / Summer Flowers
Designed for a fabric print
intricately detailed flowers are
defined by Valentina's trusty
Rapidograph ink pens.

Top / Camo
A detailed linear floral design
created for a fabric. Valentina
hand draws all her images
on watercolor paper with an
ink pen. She then scans it,
converts it into vectors and
colours it in Illustrator.

Bottom / Make Lemonade
This image was part of a food
collection Valentina made to
sell on Etsy. The lemons are
filled with intricate detail that
gives great depth and interest.

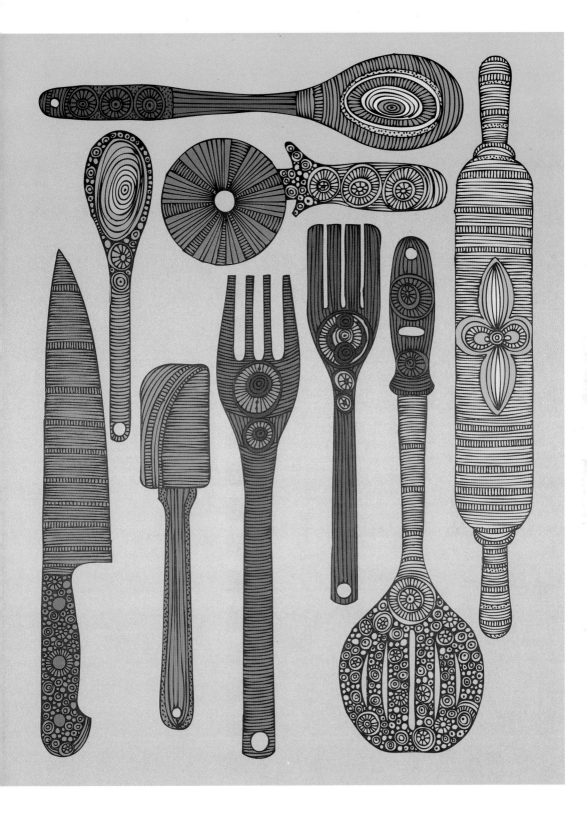

Above / In The Kitchen
Made exclusively for Pink Light Design, the image can be licensed via their studio. Valentina loves to work with different materials but black ink is one of her favourite mediums, often used as outlining and for adding the little details to her work.

Opposite / Roses
Created as a pattern for a fabric, this design is a totally unique take on a classic rose. The blooms are filled with a mixture of tiny circle motifs, dots and lines. Muted versions of the roses fill in the white spaces nicely.

Wendy MacFarlane

www.janemosse.co.uk
jane@janemosse.co.uk

100 // Wendy MacFarlane grew up in Yorkshire surrounded by the textile industry, woollen mills weaving and manufacturing. She studied Printed Textiles at Winchester School of Art and currently works as a freelance designer working with Jane Mosse designs. Wendy's main influences are a love of nature and textiles. Art School drawing projects made her see the importance of observing nature and paying attention to detail. She is always looking to create a good design in the purest form, with current pattern trends in mind. Her family is used to seeing unusual photos appear on her camera as she constantly seeks design inspiration on her travels. Snapshots of a waste bin in Vancouver, car park lines or a coffee shop menu have all gone on to inspire great pattern designs. Wendy has worked with Jane Mosse for many years selling prints all over the world (see page 126).

Design Heroes:
Matisse, Gauguin, William Morris, Klimt, the Bauhaus.

Above / Rooster Zoo
Chickens are another popular kitchen theme and this design has given them a lovely twist, incorporating peacock feathers and flourishes.

Right / Sunny Flowers
Wendy has designed a wealth of detail into this stylized floral design. Cross-hatch provides a great way to add density to flat shapes.

Above / Spice Quilt
A richly detailed floral medallion design using an earthy colour palette and folk influences creates an exotic mix.

Above / Artichokes
A stylized vegetable design which is always popular for kitchen tablecloths, curtains and aprons. Wendy has given this design interesting textures and cheerful colours.

Acknowledgements

Huge thanks to:
All the designers, studios and
artists who gave their beautiful
work to create this book; the
readers and sponsors of the
Print & Pattern website who
have helped it grow; Helen
Rochester for recognizing print
and pattern as a separate discipline
and Sophie Wise for keeping this
project in check at Laurence King;
& SMITH for their wonderful
typography and layouts.
And finally, thank you to Mum,
Dad, Mark and Lisa for all their
support and encouragement.